ENVIRONMENT AND HUMAN PERFORMANCE

Emily M. Haymes, PhD
Florida State University

and

Christine L. Wells, PhD
Arizona State University

Human Kinetics Publishers, Inc.
Champaign, IL

1258272
DLC

6-16-86 JH

Library of Congress Cataloging-in-Publication Data

Haymes, Emily M., 1939-
  Environment and human performance.

  Bibliography: p.
  Includes index.
  1. Man—Influence of environment. 2. Exercise—
Physiological aspects. 3. Adaptation (Physiology)
I. Wells, Christine L., 1938-   . II. Title.
RC1238.H39   1986   612'.04   85-22002
ISBN 0-87322-039-0

Developmental Editor: Susan Wilmoth, PhD
Production Director: Ernie Noa
Copyeditor: Terry Jopke
Typesetter: Yvonne Winsor
Text Layout: Denise Mueller
Cover Design and Layout: Jack Davis
Printed by: Braun-Brumfield, Inc.

ISBN: 0-87322-039-0

Printed in the United States of America

10 9 8 7 6 5 4 3 2 1

Human Kinetics Publishers, Inc.
Box 5076, Champaign, IL 61820

Dedication

To Elsworth R. Buskirk, PhD
Director of Noll Laboratory
The Pennsylvania State University

For stimulating our interest in environmental physiology in the first place.

Acknowledgment

Special thanks are extended to Regine Harford, Don Jones, Donna Murdoch, and Jack Winchester for their assistance in the preparation of the manuscript.

CONTENTS

Dedication   iii

Acknowledgment   v

Preface   ix

Chapter 1: THERMAL REGULATION   1

Thermal Regulation in the Human   2
Mechanisms of Temperature Regulation   3
Avenues of Heat Exchange   5
Summary   10

Chapter 2: HEAT STRESS AND PERFORMANCE   13

The Effector Mechanisms of Heat Stress   14
The Concept of Thermal Neutrality   20
The Hot Environment   20
Exercise in the Heat   22
Guidelines for Exercise Performance in the Heat   27
Acclimatization   37
Guidelines for Athletic Participation During Hot Weather   38
Summary   40

**Chapter 3: COLD ENVIRONMENTS AND HUMAN
PERFORMANCE**   43

Thermal Balance in the Cold   43

Physiological Responses to a Cold Environment   46
Exercise Responses   51
Responses to Water Immersion   54
Factors Affecting Responses to Cold   55
Acclimatization to Cold   62
Cold Injuries   64
Effects of Cold on Performance   65
Summary   68

Chapter 4: ALTITUDE AND PERFORMANCE   **69**

Physics of Altitude   70
Acute Physiological Responses   72
Responses to Exercise   77
Acclimatization to Altitude   81
Altitude Illnesses   82
Performance at Altitude   85
Return to Sea Level   88
Summary   90

Chapter 5: AIR POLLUTION AND PERFORMANCE   **93**

Air Pollutants   94
Physiological Responses to the Pollutants   99
Exercise and Air Pollutants   105
Air Pollution Mixtures   109
Pollutants and the Environment   111
Training and Performance in Polluted Environments   112
Summary   114

Chapter 6: THE TRAVELING ATHLETE   **117**

The Problem   117
Planning Ahead   118
Transmeridan Travel   121
Summary   126

**Appendix A: CALORIC VALUES FOR OXYGEN
CONSUMPTION**   **127**

**Appendix B: THE PREVENTION OF THERMAL INJURIES
DURING DISTANCE RUNNING**   **129**

References   **141**

Index   **157**

Preface

The human organism is extremely adaptable. We are capable of not only surviving in a variety of environments but of performing—sometimes incredibly well—under the most dire circumstances. We adapt to both short- and long-term exposures to the desert, the arctic, the mountains, and to transworld travel. We even tolerate air pollution.

The problems imposed by adverse environments—and our physiological solutions to them—are fascinating. The environmental aspects of human physical performance are varied and complex. Yet we have found that there are similarities among the problems in different environments.

The physiological problems encountered in adverse environments affect all systems of the body, but the greatest influence is in the cardiovascular, respiratory, renal, muscular, and neural systems. This text emphasizes both theoretical and practical aspects of these problems to encourage you to think and speculate. We also provide some straightforward answers to performance problems in adverse environments so you will understand the theoretical basis for practical solutions to real situations.

This book is intended for use by physical educators, athletes, fitness professionals, athletic trainers, physicians, health educators, physical anthropologists, and anyone else interested in human performance. Some knowledge or experience in general and/or exercise physiology is necessary. Therefore, the text is appropriate for upper-level undergraduate and initial graduate-level studies. We believe this book will provide the necessary background for more in-depth individual study in advanced graduate work. Our only desire is that you find the material as fascinating as we do.

Emily M. Haymes and
Christine L. Wells

1

Thermal Regulation

This chapter will introduce the concept of human adaptation, and begin our discussion of human response to extreme variations in environmental temperature. More specifically, this chapter will answer the following questions:

- What is a regulating organism?
- How does a regulating organism differ from a conforming organism?
- Which organ is sometimes called the human thermostat?
- Under what conditions might the hypothalamic set-point vary?
- What is an avenue of heat exchange?
- What is radiation?
- How can radiant temperature be measured?
- What factors affect the amount of heat the human body can gain or lose from radiation?
- What is the coefficient of thermal conductivity?
- Why is goose down clothing so effective in cold weather?
- What is a convective current?
- What is the latent heat of vaporization for pure water?
- What is the most significant form of evaporative heat loss from the body?
- Why is the relative humidity so important to human comfort in hot environments?

THERMAL REGULATION IN THE HUMAN

Ecology is the branch of biology that deals with the relations between living organisms and their environments. Today, it is widely recognized that an organism is at the center of an *ecosystem*. As such, it is influenced by a multitude of physical and biological environmental factors. It is the essence of living things to be part of an ecosystem and yet to be capable of resisting, to some extent, the impact of the environment (Prosser, 1964).

Organisms progress in complexity from a clump of cells that must closely conform to the conditions of their environment to more highly organized accumulations of tissues and organs that are capable of independent action. No organism's internal composition is exactly similar to its environment. Regulating organisms are capable of maintaining a relatively constant internal condition (*homeostasis*) despite widely fluctuating environmental conditions. The internal conditions of conforming organisms, on the other hand, are more closely restricted to the conditions of the surrounding environment.

The human is an excellent example of a regulating organism that is able to maintain a relatively constant internal temperature when exposed to a wide range of environmental conditions. Because of this ability, the human is referred to as a *homeotherm*, or warm-blooded animal, rather than as a *poikilotherm*, or cold-blooded animal. Regulating organisms are generally capable of living in more widely divergent environments (ecosystems) than organisms that conform to their environments.

Figure 1.1 illustrates this concept. In Figure 1.1A, the limits of survival for the organism are defined in terms of its environment. Because the organism conforms closely to its environment, it cannot survive extreme variations in that environment. In general, the *range of internal variation* tolerable to a conforming organism is somewhat greater than for a regulating organism (Prosser, 1964). In Figure 1.1B, the regulating organism does not conform to its environment but instead is capable of regulating its internal environment. As such, the regulating organism, which has a narrower internal variation, is able to survive in a wider environmental range.

The temperature of the human body oscillates in a more or less regular pattern around an average value of 37° C/98.6° F. Deep internal organs that are highly active metabolically—such as the heart, brain, liver, and kidney—have much higher temperatures than peripheral tissues. With strenuous muscular exertion, muscle temperatures rise, blood flow patterns change, and excess metabolic heat is distributed more extensively throughout the body. Body surface temperatures vary widely depending on such factors as metabolic heat load, subcutaneous blood flow patterns, ambient temperature, radiant heat load, secretion of sweat, convective air currents about the body, and relative humidity of the air. All these variables play a role in regulating body core temperature within a rather narrow range. A deep body core temperature of 41° C (106° F) is often fatal, but 42° C (107.6° F) has been tolerated for a few hours (Folk, 1974, p. 218). Heavy physical exercise has been known to elevate body core

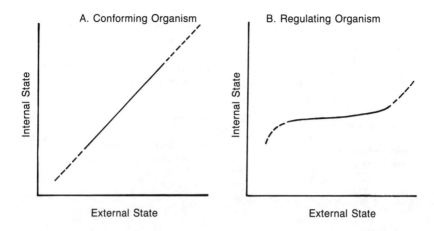

A. Conforming Organism

B. Regulating Organism

Internal State

External State

Internal State

External State

Figure 1.1 The limits of survival.

Note. Adapted from Perspectives of adaptation: Theoretical aspects (p. 13) by C.L. Prosser, 1964. In *Handbook of physiology, Section 4, Adaptation to the environment*. American Physiological Society.

temperatures to about 40° C (104° F). The lowest core temperature recorded was 17.7° C (64° F), with a respiration rate of three breaths per minute (Folk, 1974, p. 135).

MECHANISMS OF TEMPERATURE REGULATION

In humans, thermal regulation is apparently under the control of the hypothalamus. Sometimes referred to as the human thermostat, this organ is located just above the optic nerve at the base of the brain stem. The hypothalamus is thought of as the master gland of the body. In the case of temperature regulation it acts as a *thermal sensor*, an *integrator of information* from other locations in the body, and as a *controller* of various *effector mechanisms*, which are always ready to either increase or decrease the body's ability to conserve or dissipate heat. As Figure 1.2 indicates, the hypothalamus *senses* the temperature of the blood flowing through it and possibly receives information from other areas of the body.

The exact role of extrahypothalamic thermal receptor organs is controversial. Deep core receptors have been postulated but not verified in humans. Warm and cold receptors have been located in skin tissue, but there is no agreement as to their role in thermoregulation. It is possible that these receptors send information to the conscious areas of the brain to tell us about our skin temperatures but that they play a relatively unimportant role in thermoregulation. Some theoretical models give skin receptors an important role in sensory input to the hypothalamus, and others do not (Benzinger, Kinzinger & Pratt,

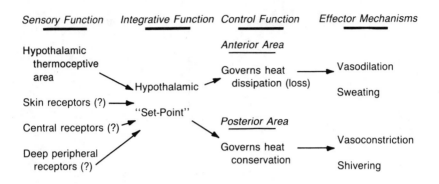

Figure 1.2 The role of the hypothalamus.

Note. From Physiological effects of a hot environment upon physical performance (p. 124) by C.L. Wells, 1980. In G.A. Stull (Ed.) *Encyclopedia of physical education, fitness and sports: Training, environment, nutrition and fitness.* Salt Lake City: Brighton Publishing Co.

1963; Hardy, 1965; Hardy, 1967). It has also been postulated but not verified, that there are peripheral receptors in the deep veins that drain the musculature.

The integrative function of the hypothalamus is thought to compare sensed information with a set-point temperature like an electrical thermostat. If the integrated information reveals that the body temperature is above the set-point, then neural discharge from the anterior area of the hypothalamus is increased, and effector mechanisms that help dissipate heat from the tissues such as vasodilation and sweating are initiated. Conversely, if the integrated sensory information reveals that the body temperature is below the set-point, then neural discharge from the posterior portion of the hypothalamus is increased, and effector mechanisms that conserve heat such as vasoconstriction and shivering are called into action. Because these two controllor areas of the hypothalamus are reciprocally innervated, we never experience both shivering and sweating at the same time. If one function is stimulated, the other function is inhibited.

The principle question about this theoretical model, of course, is: What sets the set-point? The answer is evasive. Fever is known to cause a disruption of the normal set-point. With fever, a pyrogen (a viral or bacterial agent, for example) affects the hypothalamus in some way whereby the set-point is elevated above its usual range. Antipyrogenic agents such as aspirin restore the normal set-point by destroying or inhibiting the pyrogen.

The hypothalamic set-point is not an absolute constant; it may change under many physiological and environmental conditions. For example, there are diurnal (day to night) and menstrual (follicular to luteal phase) oscillations. Several distinct circadian (about 24 hours) rhythms have been noted. A prominent pattern is a low early-morning and high late-afternoon pattern. This corresponds to the usual light-dark cycle and to the usual pattern of metabolic activity (Luce,

1971). Women have a slightly higher core temperature during the second half of the monthly menstrual cycle. This elevation in temperature may be due to the anabolic effects of progesterone, but the exact mechanism is unknown.

Before examining the physiological role of the effector mechanisms in temperature regulation, we will discuss the physical avenues of heat exchange. These are the physical processes by which heat can be transferred or transported from one tissue to another, from one space to another, from the environment to the body, or conversely, from the body to the environment.

AVENUES OF HEAT EXCHANGE

Thermal balance can best be understood by the law of conservation of energy. Simply, this law states that for a system to be in thermal balance, all avenues of heat gain or loss must quantitatively balance to zero. This can be expressed by the following formula:

$$M \pm R \pm K \pm C - E \pm W \pm S = 0 \text{ or thermal balance}$$

where M = metabolic heat production

R = radiative heat exchange

K = conductive heat exchange

C = convective heat exchange

E = evaporative heat loss

W = work accomplished (negative for work against external forces and positive for work against internal forces)

S = heat storage (negative for heat storage, i.e., body temperature gain, and positive for heat loss)

For an individual at rest, $W = 0$. If the individual is in a state of thermal equilibrium, $S = 0$. Let's examine each part of the equation in more detail.

Metabolic Heat Production

Metabolic heat production (M) is the body's only means of heat production and as such is really not an avenue of heat exchange. It is the total energy released by all anaerobic and aerobic processes and is most often determined by measuring oxygen uptake, calculating the respiratory exchange ratio (R = $\dot{V}CO_2/\dot{V}O_2$), and multiplying by the appropriate kilocalorie factor for consumed oxygen (see Appendix A). (For example, if $\dot{V}O_2$ is 3.02 L•min^{-1} and R = 0.89, then the metabolic heat production equals 3.02 L•min^{-1} × 4.91 kcal•L^{-1} of O_2 = 14.83 kcal•min^{-1}). Metabolic heat production can be elevated voluntarily by exercise and involuntarily by shivering. Some persons can lower their metabolic heat production by entering a deep meditative state, but most of us have not developed our capacity to do so.

Radiation

Radiation (R) is the exchange of electromagnetic energy waves emitted from one object and absorbed by another. The solar heat gain on a clear summer day is the most obvious example of radiant heat exchange. Another example is the loss of heat from the earth on a clear cool night. Radiative heat exchange can be expressed as follows:

$$R = \sigma (T_s^4 - T_R^4) \, A_r$$
where R   = radiation
σ = Stefan-Boltzmann constant = 5.67×10^{-8} R $\times$ m^{-2} $\times$ K^{-1}
T_s = average surface temperature
T_R = average radiant temperature
A_r = effective radiant surface area

Globe temperature is often used to measure radiant temperature (T_R). A 6-in. diameter copper sphere painted flat black is suspended with a thermometer sealed inside so that the sensory section is located exactly in the center. The black globe represents an "ideal black body," which is an object that absorbs all the radiation that falls on it. The emittance of a black body is by definition equal to 1 in all temperatures. The emittance of a nonblack body varies with temperature. The human body is very close to an ideal black body, because it absorbs nearly all the radiation that falls on it. For that reason it is a good idea to be lightly but fully clothed when directly exposed to sunlight. Clothed individuals sitting in the sun gain only about half as much heat as unclothed persons. Desert clothing has traditionally been white, which reflects *more* heat and absorbs *less* heat than does the skin or dark-colored clothing. Skin color has been reported to affect the amount of solar radiation absorbed. White skin reflects 30% to 45% of the solar radiation in the visible and ultraviolet ranges of the spectrum, whereas black skin reflects less than 19% of these rays (Frisancho, 1979, p. 14). The surface of a substance also affects its ability to reflect or to absorb heat. Smooth surfaces absorb more heat than do rough surfaces. These factors are reflected in the Stefan-Boltzmann constant in the formula. The effective radiating surface area of a person standing with arms and legs spread is approximately 85% of the total skin area. In the sitting position, it is approximately 70% to 75% of the total body surface area.

Conduction

Conduction (K) of heat occurs whenever two surfaces with differing temperatures are in direct contact. The transfer of heat energy from one substance to another is directly related to the difference in temperature between the two (the thermal gradient or ΔT). It is also a direct function of the thermal conductivity (k) of each substance. *Conductors* are substances that conduct heat readily. *Insulators* (nonconductors) are substances that do not conduct heat readily. Metals are good conductors, whereas nonmetals are better insulators. Still air is an excellent insulator, whereas water is an excellent conductor. This explains why a naked body experiences greater thermal stress in 10° C (50° F) water than in 10° C air. Fat tissue is a better insulator than muscle tissues. Therefore, a fatter person loses less heat when immersed in cold water than a leaner subject. The rate of conductive heat exchange is inversely related to the thickness of the insulating substance. This is why the thick layer of still air trapped in goose down clothing is so effective in cold weather and why the layer principle of dressing for the cold is advocated. Conductive heat exchange can be expressed as follows:

$$K = (k/d) (T_1 - T_2) A_k$$

where K = conduction

k = coefficient of thermal conductivity

d = thickness of substance

$T_1 - T_2$ = temperature gradient between two substances or surfaces

A_k = area of contact

Conductive heat loss represents only a small percentage of the total heat exchange between the body and the environment. Thus, conduction is usually not considered separately but is discussed in conjunction with radiation and convection. The area of skin in contact with external objects is usually small, and people usually avoid direct contact with highly conductive materials. However, body heat is conducted from skin to clothing. When body heat reaches the clothing, it is dissipated from the outer clothing surfaces by evaporation, convection, or radiation depending on the vapor pressure, air movement, and the skin-clothing-ambient temperature gradients.

Convection

Convection (C) or convection heat exchange requires that one of the media be moving, as occurs with a fluid or gaseous medium. This is referred to as a convective current. Heat is transported by a stream of molecules from a warm object toward a cooler object. Convection can be expressed as follows:

$$C = k_c (T_1 - T_2) A_c$$

where C = convection

k_c = surface coefficient of convection heat transfer

A_c = effective area of convection heat exchange

The coefficient of convective heat transfer is a function of the convective current, the viscosity and density of the medium, and the thermal conductivity of the substances involved. Convection is directly related to the temperature gradient between the substances as well as to the effective convective surface area and surface coefficient at each boundary layer. An example of convective heat exchange is the devastating effect of high winds on a cool day (wind chill factor). Convective heat exchange can occur *within* the human body as well. When warmed blood from metabolically active areas of the body flows past cooled blood from the periphery of the body, the warmed blood is cooled, and the cooled blood is warmed. This is known as countercurrent heat exchange. This phenomenon can become complicated during exercise. The most common exchange of body heat by convection begins with heat conduction from a warm body to surrounding air molecules. The heated air expands, becomes less dense, and rises—taking heat with it. The area immediately adjacent to the skin is then replaced by cooler, denser air, and the process is repeated.

Evaporation

Evaporation (E) occurs when water changes from a liquid to a gas. For this to happen, heat must be supplied (note that heat can never be gained via evaporation and hence the sign is always negative). The thermal energy required is called the *latent heat of vaporization* and equals 580 calories per gram of distilled-deionized water. For human sweat this value is lower because of electrolytes in the fluid. Evaporative heat loss is directly related to the heat of vaporization and to the amount of liquid vaporized (evaporated). In the human body, evaporative heat losses occur as a result of insensible perspiration (diffusion of water through the skin), thermal and nonthermal (nervous) sweating, and water losses from the respiratory tract during respiration. A man at rest who is comfortably warm loses water from his respiratory tract and by insensible perspiration at a rate of about 30 gm per hr (Carlson & Hsieh, 1974, p. 63). Higher respiratory rates or very low relative humidity may significantly increase this value. High environmental temperatures and/or strenuous exercise may result in thermal sweating rates as high as 1.5 to 2.0 liters per hr.

Evaporative heat losses from the respiratory tract are usually not significant. However, under such conditions as high altitude and/or extremely cold and dry air, evaporative heat losses from respiration can become physiologically significant. The amount of heat lost by respiration can be expressed as follows:

$$E_{res} = 40 \ \dot{V}_E \ (D_{ex} - \phi \ D_{in})$$

where E_{Resp} = heat loss via the respiratory tract

$\dot{V}_E$ = ventilation volume in $L \cdot min^{-1}$

D_{ex} = density of saturated exhaled air $(gm \cdot min^{-1})$

D_{in} = density of saturated inhaled air $(gm \cdot min^{-1})$

ϕ = fractional relative humidity.

(Adapted from Carlson and Hsieh, 1974)

The density of saturated air varies with temperature. Relative humidity is a function of how much water the air can hold at a given environmental temperature. Everyone knows that evaporation is very slow in areas of high relative humidity. That is why hot, humid environments are so much more stressful than hot, dry environments.

Evaporative heat losses from the skin surface depend primarily on three factors. One is the rate of evaporation, which is dependent on the relative humidity of the surrounding air and the amount of air movement across the skin. A second factor is the rate of sweat secretion from the sweat glands. The third factor is the latent heat of evaporation for the sweat secreted, which varies with the electrolyte concentration of the sweat. Heat losses from the skin can be approximated by the following:

$$E_{sw} = 40 \, h_D \, (P_{ws} - \phi P_{wa}) \, /R_w \, T$$

where E_{sw} = the rate of heat loss from sweating

h_D = transfer coefficient (L•min^{-1})

ϕ = fractional realtive humidity

P_{ws} = vapor pressure of water at skin temperature (mm Hg)

P_{wa} = vapor pressure of water at ambient temperature

R_w = aqueous gas constant

T = average of skin and ambient temperature (K)

(Adapted from Carlson and Hsieh, 1974)

Most often evaporative heat losses are determined by carefully measuring the total amount of water lost from the body per unit of time. This is done by calculating total weight loss and correcting for fluid intake and the weight of excess carbon dioxide produced.

The roles played by the four avenues of heat exchange depend on the interactions between the ambient temperature, the relative humidity, and the core-skin temperature gradient. This is partially shown in Table 1. Simply, in a comfortable climate of 25° C, a seated nude person loses heat mostly by radiation (67%) and evaporation (23%). In a warmer climate of about 30° C, radiative losses decrease slightly, and convective losses increase. At temperatures higher than 35° C, little body heat can be lost via radiation and convection, and evaporative heat losses become extremely important. In the event that vapor pressure is high (high relative humidity), then the evaporation of sweat is minimal, and heat tolerance is limited.

Recently some interesting innovations have occurred in clothing design concepts for cold weather. Using "breathable" external fabrics and carefully designed venting in the underarm, back, wrist, and ankle areas, the concept of layering with polypropylene undergarments is gaining popularity. "Vapor barrier" clothing is designed to rid the body of perspiration and dampness without losing heat by evaporation. Mountaineers, backpackers, hunters, and

Table 1.1

The Partitioning of Actual Heat Loss to the Environment

Room Temperature	Radiation	Convection	Evaporation
Comfortable (25° C)	67%	10%	23%
Warm (30° C)	41%	33%	26%
Hot (35° C)	4%	6%	90%

Note. From Textbook of environmental physiology, 2nd edition (p. 111) by G.E. Folk, 1974, Philadelphia: Lea Febiger. Reprinted with permission.

cross-country skiers are aware that strenuous exertion in the cold generates plenty of body heat and sweat. When one stops, slows down, or encounters high winds, the loss of heat via evaporation can be extremely chilling and even life-threatening. Vapor barrier clothing is supposed to end all this by "wicking" the body's excess moisture to the surface of the clothing for evaporation while retaining the body's heat. Although it sounds like a great idea and it sometimes works, not all the problems have been solved. Under some conditions, vapor barrier clothing can create an internal heat stress of its own. Nevertheless, it is an excellent example of an attempt to apply our knowledge of the physical avenues of heat exchange to our practical advantage.

Now that the general concepts of thermal regulation have been discussed, we can move to more specific situations involving the physiological mechanisms for resisting and adjusting to the stresses imposed by our environment. Chapter 2 will elaborate on the human response to heat stress.

SUMMARY

As a regulating organism, the human is able to maintain a relatively constant internal temperature within a wide range of environmental conditions. Conforming organisms, on the other hand, cannot survive extreme environmental variations as readily.

Thermal regulation is under the control of the hypothalamus which acts much like a room thermostat. It senses temperature information from various sources and directs the body's responses in relation to an internal set-point temperature. Effector mechanisms mediate the conservation or dissipation of internal body heat accordingly.

The physical avenues of heat exchange include radiation, conduction, convection, and radiation. To maintain thermal equilibrium, the body must quantitatively balance these factors in relation to metabolic heat production and environmental stressors. Radiative heat gain occurs whenever radiant temperature exceeds average body surface temperature. Conductive heat exchange occurs when two surfaces in direct contact differ in temperature. Transfer of heat from one surface to another is directly related to the thermal conductivity of the substances. Water is an excellent conductor of heat whereas still air is an excellent insulator. Convective heat exchange requires a moving medium. A cold wind blowing past a warm body can have a devastating effect on body temperature. Evaporative heat losses can occur from the respiratory tract and from the skin surface. Heat loss via this avenue of exchange is significantly affected by the relative humidity of the surrounding air. An understanding of the basic principles of heat exchange is of practical significance in knowing how to protect oneself from harsh environmental conditions.

2

Heat Stress and Performance

This chapter will focus on human adaptation to heat stress. We will discuss basic physiological mechanisms of response and adaptation as well as implications for performance in hot environments. The following questions will be discussed:

- How does the distribution of blood flow control heat loss from the body?
- What are the secondary consequences of vasodilatation?
- From what body compartment does most eccrine or thermal sweat come?
- What does the statement, "Sweat is hypotonic to plasma," mean?
- What role does the kidney play in the regulation of sweating?
- What are the ideal environmental conditions for exercise in the heat?
- How is the temperature gradient between the deep tissues and the skin surface affected by the sun?
- What happens to the temperature gradient between the deep tissues and the skin when sweat does *not* evaporate because of high humidity?
- Why does one's cardiovascular fitness level play such a large role in heat tolerance?
- Are there sexual differences in heat tolerance?
- Are young children more susceptible to heat injury than adults?
- What is the WBGT index?
- How devastating is dehydration to human performance?
- How can dehydration be prevented?
- What substances are lost in human sweat?
- Should you drink electrolyte replacement fluids during competition?
- What are some of the physiological changes seen with heat acclimatization?

We have described the physical means by which heat can be exchanged (avenues of heat exchange), and we have described the control mechanisms by which internal temperature can be regulated (mechanisms of temperature regulation). Heat dissipation is the fundamental problem for regulating organisms exposed to heat stress. Successful tolerance of heat stress requires coordinated responses that facilitate heat loss to maintain homeostasis. We will now discuss the role of the physiological effector mechanisms of heat stress and how they relate to the topics already discussed.

THE EFFECTOR MECHANISMS OF HEAT STRESS

Vasodilatation

The anterior portion of the hypothalamus regulates blood flow through the deep and superficial vessels of the body. The hypothalamus sends neural commands to the vasomotor center in the brain stem and directly affects the smooth muscles of the metarterioles that control the flow of blood between deep and superficial vessels. By directing warm blood from the core of the body to the surface layers, body heat can be dissipated from one group of tissues to another and in some instances eliminated from the body. The core-shell concept is a particularly important one to understand. Figure 2.1 describes this dynamic mechanism.

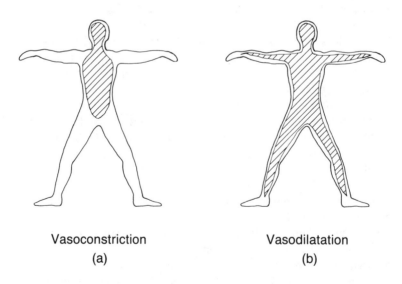

Vasoconstriction   Vasodilatation
(a)   (b)

Figure 2.1 The core-shell concept.

The essential organs of the body include the brain, heart, lungs, liver, and kidneys (Figure 2.1A). It is important that these organs, which are very active metabolically, are protected from extreme losses of body heat under cold environmental conditions. These organs and surrounding tissues are referred to as the body core, and they always receive a large supply of blood. Under certain conditions, however, these organs must also be protected from high body temperatures. For example, when the body is exposed to extremely high environmental temperatures, heat must be removed from the body to prevent tissue damage (particularly to the brain). Even without exposure to high environmental temperatures, the body can become severely overheated—for example, during prolonged and strenuous exercise in a humid environment. By directing blood flow away from the core tissues to the peripheral tissues, it is possible to redistribute and/or to remove heat that could be deleterious to survival. By diverting blood flow from deep to superficial vessels (Figure 2.1B), heat can be transferred to other tissues (conduction, convection) or transferred to the environment (conduction, radiation). The principal factor involved here is the temperature gradient (ΔT) between the blood and the surrounding tissues and between the skin and the surrounding environment. If the shell (the peripheral tissues) is cooler than the core (the deeper tissues), heat will be exchanged and the core will cool down. This is, of course, a very dynamic mechanism that is under constant adjustment and control. As long as the body surface layers are cooler than the external temperatures, heat can be lost via radiation, conduction, or convection. If the environmental heat load is so extreme that the skin surface becomes as warm or warmer than the core temperature, then heat will be gained from the environment and internal heat can no longer be exchanged via these mechanisms.

Secondary Consequences of Vasodilatation

Vasodilatation plays an important role in regulating body temperature during exercise and environmental heat stress. Nevertheless, this valuable effector mechanism can also cause some significant physiological problems. With increased blood flow to the peripheral tissues, blood flow to other areas of the body must decrease. There is, after all, only a finite amount of blood available. When the body is suddenly forced to distribute 5 or 6 L of blood over a vascular area that may suddenly double or triple in size, some immediate adjustments must be made. Central blood pressure must be maintained. One mechanism is for blood flow to decrease in certain less-necessary organs and tissues. For example, renal and splanchnic blood flow usually decrease during heat stress. The corresponding decline in urine excretion conserves plasma water. Digestive processes also slow down.

Another physiological adjustment to vasodilatation is an immediate increase in cardiac output ($\dot{Q}$). Cardiac output is a function of the heart rate (HR) and the stroke volume (SV) of the heart ($\dot{Q} = HR \times SV$). The increase in cardiac output accompanying vasodilatation is effected by a sometimes dramatic increase in heart rate. Persons exposed to high environmental heat often have near-maximal heart rates—even with mild exercise or rest. Because cutaneous blood vessels may not be affected by the exercise and are characterized by low blood pressures, venous return usually decreases considerably when vasodilatation occurs because of heat stress. Consequently, the stroke volume may decrease significantly. This means that the heart rate is the primary mechanism for maintaining cardiac output. In the heat, one often experiences general weakness, which is probably related to the deprivation of blood (oxygen and fuel) to the muscles and a corresponding fall in arterial blood pressure. Some people, in the heat, experience tunnel vision (a narrowing of peripheral vision), which is probably a manifestation of this.

If vasodilatation is extreme (much blood going to the periphery and little remaining in the core), one may experience cardiac insufficiency or compromise. This is especially prevalent among obese, elderly, and sedentary people, and during periods of heavy exercise in extremely high environmental temperatures.

Sweating

Sweating is an effective means by which to lose body heat. However, heat is lost only if evaporation occurs. When the ambient temperature exceeds the skin temperature ($T_a > T_{sk}$), the temperature gradient favors heat gain, and evaporation of sweat is the only mechanism by which the body can dissipate internal heat. Under such conditions, radiation, conduction, and convection will result in body heat gain. When relative humidity is high or when there is insufficient air flow past the skin surface, evaporation is limited. When both air temperature and relative humidity are high, the body will soon reach its limit of heat tolerance.

There are two types of sweat glands. Both are found in the dermal layer of the skin just above the subcutaneous tissue. Apocrine glands secret a watery substance that contains lipid molecules, has a trace of color, and has a slightly musky odor. These glands are found predominantly on the palms of the hands, the soles of the feet, the armpits, and the groin. They are also sometimes found on the face, particularly in the area of the upper lip. Apocrine sweat is known as nervous or emotional sweat, because it is secreted in response to various neurochemical stimuli and not by thermal stress. Eccrine sweat glands, on the other hand, are distributed more evenly about the body, although several distinct sweat gland distribution patterns have been reported (Kuno, 1956).

Eccrine sweat is the primary topic of this section, because this is the so-called thermal sweat. These glands are under the direct control of the anterior portion of the hypothalamus. Stimulation of this portion of the master gland results in sweating and the increased production of a clear, watery, odorless fluid, which is an ultrafiltrate of blood plasma. Thermal sweat glands can also be stimulated by the effects of radiant heat applied to the skin (Bullard et al., 1967, 1968). Sweating in response to heat stress is usually very rapid and effective. Much body heat can be lost if evaporation is sufficient and the skin surface remains reasonably dry. There is considerable evidence to suggest that sweating gradually declines if the skin surface becomes thoroughly wet.

Secondary Consequences of Sweating

As with vasodilatation, a number of physiological events occur secondary to significant thermal sweating. One event is a shift of body fluid from the interstitial space to the vascular bed. This occurs so rapidly that blood volume may actually increase temporarily. Because thermal sweat comes from the plasma water, this fluid shifts so that the blood will not become concentrated too rapidly. Only after prolonged periods of sweating does blood concentration become a serious problem to the well-hydrated individual. When that occurs, intracellular water shifts into the extracellular space so that sweating can be maintained, but the body tissues may become severely dehydrated. Figure 2.2 provides a quick review of the fluid compartments of the body.

Because sweat is an ultrafiltrate of plasma water, it possesses almost everything that is found in blood except the plasma proteins. Nevertheless, sweat is hypotonic (less concentrated) to the plasma water, and therefore, the substances are found in lesser concentrations. The major elements in sweat are the extracellular electrolytes sodium (Na^+) and chloride (Cl^-), and the intracellular electrolyte potassium (K^+). Other components in sweat include urea, lactic acid, CO_2, PO_4, Mg^+, nitrogen, bicarbonate (HCO_3), iron, and zinc. Some water-soluble vitamins are probably also lost in sweat.

Because sweat is hypotonic to plasma water, the major substance lost from the body is water. Nevertheless, many people are concerned about electrolyte losses and advocate glucose and electrolyte replacement solutions (Gatorade, ERG, Braketime, Body Punch, etc.) during sport or work situations in which large amounts of water are lost. However, because the sweat glands effective-

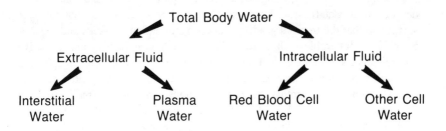

Figure 2.2 Body water compartments.

ly conserve the body components, there is probably too much emphasis on electrolyte replacement and not enough emphasis on fluid (water) replacement. Far more solvent (water) is lost from the body than solutes (substances). Fluid and electrolyte replacement will be discussed more thoroughly.

Decreased urinary output is another consequence of prolonged or profuse sweating. This is, of course, a protective response against a severe loss of blood volume. The kidney vigorously regulates water balance. Whenever fluid losses threaten to upset water balance, arterial blood pressure declines, which decreases renal blood flow and glomerular filtration rate. Under these conditions, urine output is held to a minimum. In addition, because sweat is hypotonic to the body fluids, plasma osmolarity is elevated with prolonged sweat losses. Elevated osmolarity elicits an increase in the secretion of antidiuretic hormone (ADH) from the pituitary. ADH acts on the tubules of the kidney, causing increased reabsorption of water and a consequent water conservation. Electrolyte excretion by the kidneys is coupled with the regulation of water balance. When sweating rates are high, the kidney conserves Na^+ by increasing the reabsorption of that electrolyte at the site of the distal tubule. The steroid hormone, aldosterone, from the adrenal cortex plays a significant role in this mechanism as does decreased arterial blood pressure. Figure 2.3 presents some of the pathways by which sodium and water are conserved in response to severe sweating.

Prolonged and profuse sweating can result in circulatory distress. To the extent that fluids are not adequately replaced during heat stress, water losses can lead to dehydration. If fluid losses are sufficient to cause an increase in the viscosity of the blood (decreased plasma volume), then the strain on the heart can become severe. In this event, heart rate will be very high, stroke volume will decline considerably, and the individual is likely to suffer syncope (fainting) and even become comatose. Elderly, obese, and sedentary people, and people with heart disease are particularly susceptible.

Other Mechanisms of Body Heat Loss

Vasodilatation and sweating are usually observed together. Both mechanisms occur simultaneously and are somewhat dependent upon each other. Vasodilatation, of course, brings an increased supply of blood (and water) to the dermal sweat glands, and the evaporation of sweat serves to cool the skin surface so that the thermal gradient between surrounding tissues and the ambient air is favorable to heat loss. There are few additional and effective mechanisms. With an elevated body temperature (hyperthermia), respiration rate and respiration volume usually increase. Because relatively little heat can be lost from the respiratory tract, this response has only a small effect on temperature regulation. In fact, elevated minute ventilation ($\dot{V}_E$, $L \cdot min^{-1}$) is likely to cause hyperventilation, a corresponding decrease in the partial pressure of carbon dioxide (PCO_2), respiratory alkalosis, and syncope.

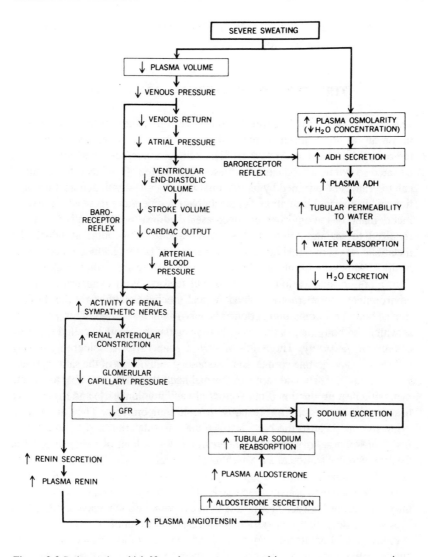

Figure 2.3 Pathways by which Na and water are conserved in response to severe sweating.

Note. From Human physiology: The mechanisms of body function (2nd ed.) (p. 344) by J.H. Vander, J.H. Sherman, and D.S. Luciano, 1975, New York: McGraw-Hill. Reprinted with permission.

Additional mechanisms are not physiological but behavioral in nature. When people are exposed to heat stress they usually make conscious efforts to enhance heat loss or to prevent heat gain. These behavioral alterations include selecting lightweight and light-colored clothing, removing or adjusting clothing to allow for better ventilation, resting in the shade, drinking water, decreasing work rate, and planning the activities to avoid discomfort.

THE CONCEPT OF THERMAL NEUTRALITY

The concept of thermal neutrality comes from the study of the changes that occur in a homeotherm's physiological responses when environmental temperature is varied. At low ambient temperatures, the metabolic rate is elevated so that heat production increases. The degree of cold that the organism can tolerate is determined by its maximal rate of cold-stimulated heat production and its thermal insulation. As the ambient temperature increases, the thermal demand of the environment decreases, and heat production is no longer required to maintain internal body temperature. The point at which the metabolic rate is minimal depends on a number of factors including body composition (fatness, muscularity, linearity, body surface area), diet, acclimatization, clothing, and various environmental factors. With exposure to higher environmental temperatures, physiological mechanisms that aid the dissipation of body heat come into action. The environmental range of temperatures at which the body makes the least thermoregulatory effort is called the *zone of thermal neutrality*. The width of such a zone varies considerably among different homeothermic species and also among individuals of the same species. Humans have a fairly wide zone of thermal neutrality. They are able to elevate metabolic heat production (both voluntarily and involuntarily) and to conserve heat via vasoconstriction in response to cold temperatures. They are able to bring internal heat to the body surface via vasodilatation and to sweat profusely in response to warm temperatures. The lower limit of the zone is set at the environmental temperature at which metabolic heat production first rises (a resting body is assumed), and the upper limit of the zone is set by the onset of sweating and increased evaporative heat loss. This concept allows us to study the relationships between heat production, evaporative and nonevaporative heat losses, and deep body temperatures in response to ambient exposure.

Figure 2.4 illustrates the concept of thermal neutrality. Vasodilatation occurs at some point above the critical temperature. This facilitates an increase in the transfer of heat from the core to the surface; that is, it increases thermal conductance through body tissues. The critical temperature is the lower end of the zone of minimal metabolism. Below this ambient temperature, mechanisms of heat conservation must be used to maintain internal body temperature (Ingram & Mount 1975, p. 26).

THE HOT ENVIRONMENT

Humans encounter heat stress in tropical zones surrounding the equator and during summer months in the temperate zones. Hot climates can generally be classi-

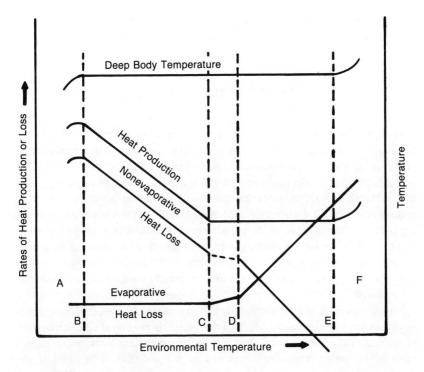

Figure 2.4. The zone of thermal neutrality.

Note. From *Man and animals in hot environments* (p. 26) by D.L. Ingram and L.E. Mount, 1975, New York: Springer Verlag. Reprinted with permission.
A = zone of hypothermia; B = temperature of peak metabolism and incipient hypothermia; C = critical temperature; D = temperature of marked increase in evaporative heat; E = temperature of incipient hyperthermia; F = zone of hyperthermia; CD = zone of least thermoregulatory effort and minimal demand; CE = zone of minimal metabolism; BE = thermoregulatory range.

fied either as hot-dry or hot-wet. Hot-dry atmospheres are found in the various deserts of the world. These climates are characterized by high air temperatures (32° to 52° C or 99° to 125° F), low humidity (0% to 15% relative humidity), and intense solar radiation. Because there is little precipitation, there is little vegetation. There is usually also considerable day-night variation in temperature because of the radiation of ground heat back to the dark sky at night. The high solar load and high air and ground temperatures of the desert prevent body heat loss via radiation, conduction, and convection, but the low moisture content favors heat loss via evaporation which is therefore the primary thermal regulatory effector mechanism.

In the tropical and subtropical rain forests, the climate is characterized by air temperatures that seldom exceed 35° C (95° F) and usually range from 27° to 32° C (80° to 90° F). The average relative humidity usually exceeds 50%, however, and there is marked seasonal precipitation. Vegetation is abundant, and this provides ample shade. In this sort of climate, evaporation is limited, and little body heat can be lost via the sweating mechanism.

EXERCISE IN THE HEAT

A resting person produces about 75 kcal per hour of metabolic heat. When exercise begins, heat production increases in a corresponding manner. With prolonged or intense exercise, metabolic heat production can be elevated some 20-fold, to about 1,500 kcal per hour. It is obvious that this extra heat must be dissipated, or body temperature will rapidly rise above normal levels. Even without environmental heat stress, this internal heat load will eventually become a problem. It is common for deep body core temperatures to range from 38° to 41° C (100° to 106° F) during periods of exercise. To perform strenuous exercise under climatic conditions that prevent the almost-immediate loss of body heat or that add an external heat load immensely compounds the physiological problems.

With the increase of muscular activity, oxygen uptake increases, ATP is broken down, and energy is released. Much of this energy is not bound up in mechanical or cellular work. Instead it is lost as heat to the surrounding cells, which include other muscle tissues, connective tissues, and the cells and fluids of the blood stream. Consequently, there is a general heating of the surrounding areas. Because this would elevate deep temperatures in relation to surface (skin) temperatures, the ensuing temperature gradient would favor the loss of deep body heat via the mechanisms of radiation, conduction, and convection. In addition, muscular contraction almost immediately stimulates thermal sweating. If sweat secretions evaporate, skin temperature declines, which further increases the temperature gradient between the deep tissues and the skin surface. As described so far, then, temperature regulation ought to be no problem whatsoever. And that is the case as long as the surrounding air remains cool, the solar load is not excessive, and evaporation keeps up with sweat secretion. In short, there is little problem with body temperature regulation during exercise under ideal environmental conditions such as cool air temperatures, moderate air flow, and low vapor pressure. However, if even one of these variables changes, the task of adequately regulating the deep body core temperature is magnified considerably.

For example, let's assume that the solar heat load is increased so that the body begins to gain heat via radiation. As surface tissues gradually heat up, the temperature gradient situation discussed above ($T_{deep\ tissues} > T_{surface\ tissues}$) is reduced, or even reversed; that is, the temperatures of the surface tissues become equal to or even greater than the temperatures of the deep tissues. This means that the methods of dissipating the increased metabolic heat of muscle contraction are seriously jeopardized. Deep body heat is no longer able to flow to the surface for release to the environment. Now the body must rely exclusively on the sweat mechanism and the evaporative power of the environment for removal of excess metabolic heat.

Another example is also relevant. Often our exercise environment is only moderately warm (21° to 26° C or 70° to 80° F) but rather humid (50% to 95% relative humidity). In this situation, the evaporative power of the environment is not very high, and body sweat accumulates on the skin surface. Without sufficient evaporation, the skin temperature gradually rises. Here again the temperature gradient between the deep tissues and the surface tissues becomes smaller and smaller, and body heat loss is retarded. Without the constant removal of metabolic heat, deep body temperature will rise almost immediately. Exercise tolerance under such a condition could be limited depending on one's environmental acclimatization.

Convective heat dissipation within the body is also affected by exercise and increased metabolic heat load. Countercurrent heat exchange was described under normal resting conditions. With exercise, considerable body heat may be produced in the peripheral tissues—that is, in the muscles of the limbs. In such a situation, venous blood temperature becomes elevated, perhaps even higher than that of the arterial blood supply coming into the limb from the deep tissues. Rather than heat flow from the arterial blood warming the cooler venous blood and vice versa, the heat flow is from the heated venous blood to the already warm arterial blood. In this event, peripherally produced metabolic heat is being carried to the body core. To the extent that this condition occurs, exercise tolerance will be limited.

The ability to tolerate strenuous exercise in the heat is probably determined more by one's cardiovascular efficiency than by any single physiological factor. With exercise, the active muscle cells require an increased amount of oxygen and metabolic substrate. In addition, more carbon dioxide and possibly lactic acid and ammonia are produced. These waste substances must be removed. The circulatory system serves as the major transport system for these and other components of metabolism. In a cool or cold environment there is little problem with increasing blood flow to the active muscle cells. Under conditions of elevated heat load, however, the circulatory system must also increase the blood supplied to the skin and subcutaneous tissues. In fact, at work loads above about 1 L•min^{-1} of oxygen, there is usually an increase in cutaneous as well as muscle blood flow. In a cool, dry environment, probably about 70% of the heat loss during exercise is due to radiation and convection, and about 30% is lost as a result of evaporation (Åstrand and Rodahl, 1977). In this situation, skin temperatures usually decrease because of the cooling effect of the evaporation of sweat. Skin temperatures do not usually increase during exercise except under hot, humid conditions.

The more stressful the exercise environment, the more cutaneous blood flow occurs. This means, of course, that less blood is available for the muscles. Less blood flow also means less oxygen, less substrate, and less removal of metabolic waste products. The person who is less cardiovascularly fit will first experience the sensation of heavy limbs, then extreme fatigue, dizziness, nausea, tunnel vision, and finally collapse. The more cardiovascularly fit individual will be better able to supply blood to the muscles as well as to the cutaneous layers. In addition, highly trained subjects have an earlier onset of sweating and a heightened sweating response. All this means more body cooling, less physiological stress, and better exercise performance. The fitter, endurance-trained individual will be more capable of maintaining venous return. Because of this, stroke volume will not fall as much, heart rate will not be as elevated, and cardiac output will be maintained or elevated for a longer period.

Because of the alterations in blood flow, oxygen uptake at the active muscle site is diminished. Because the total blood flow to the active muscles is reduced, the muscles are shortchanged in terms of oxygen delivery and waste product removal. This usually results in an accumulation of lactic acid and a reduction in maximal oxygen uptake in the heat. This is the major cause of the decline in work performance in hot-dry and hot-humid environments.

There are also psychological and motivational factors involved in exercise tolerance in the heat. For some persons, the physical discomforts are so psychologically devastating that they will stop exercising before they reach their physiological limitations.

Sexual Differences in Heat Tolerance

Early research indicated that women had poor tolerance to exercise in the heat. Careful examination of this research showed that the results were largely dependent on the subjects chosen for study. In most cases these early studies compared young male army trainees with somewhat older, fatter, and less-active army nurses. The male soldiers were either in training or had just completed boot camp training. The women nurses, although on their feet a great deal as a result of their employment, were not particularly fit. The most important physiological factor in regard to one's ability to tolerate heat, and particularly exercise in the heat, is cardiovascular efficiency, and it is obvious that the army nurses were not nearly as cardiovascularly fit as the young men after training camp. In addition, the men and women in these studies were always assigned some sort of standardized work task (either walking on a treadmill at a given speed and grade or riding a bicycle ergometer at a given resistance). Because the women were not as fit as the men, they were exercising harder in relation to their capacity than the men. No wonder they did not do so well. One study during these early years of investigation of heat tolerance used more fit women, and the results of that study differed from the others. This study indicated that women were as able as men to exercise in the heat (Weinman et al., 1967). More recent studies (Paolone, Wells, & Kelly, 1977; Wells, 1977; Wells & Paolone, 1977) that assigned exercise tasks on the basis of percentage of individual maximal oxygen uptake and that had subjects who had more similar cardiovascular efficiency indicated that the women tolerated heat at least as well as the men.

Several observations about women exercising in the heat have been verified, however. One is that women do not generally sweat as much as men, even though they have as many sweat glands. One well-known investigator even refers to the male as a "wasteful, prolific sweater," while he describes the female as able to adjust her "sweat rate better to the required heat loss" (Wyndham et al., 1965). It has been suggested that the sex hormones account for this difference (Kawahata, 1960). The reasoning was that because testosterone is anabolic in nature, it stimulates sweating, and because estrogen is catabolic, that it inhibits sweating. So far, however, this has not been satisfactorily demonstrated. Wells and Horvath (1973, 1974) postulated that if the female hormones were responsible for lower sweat production, the cyclic variations in sweating response should occur during different hormonal phases of the menstrual cycle. However, they found no significant differences in heat responses. Although luteal phase sweating (onset of sweating) and evaporative rates tended to lag behind values during the other two menstrual phases when estrogen values were higher, the values were essentially the same after 40 minutes of heat exposure. Sargent and Weinman (1966) also failed to detect differences in sweat gland activity during phases of the menstrual cycle. And so, the fact that women generally do not seem to sweat as much as do men remains unexplained.

Another sexual difference in heat stress response that has been noted by many investigators is the higher heart rates in women during heat exposure. Because women also have higher skin temperatures than men, the assumption is that women have a lesser venous return to the heart as a result of a higher cutaneous blood flow. This would indicate that women exercising in the heat have a smaller stroke volume at a given cardiac output than men.

Women capable of sustaining a high heart rate in the face of a lesser venous return will be as able as men to tolerate heat stress. Recent research indicates that the cardiovascularly fit woman is capable of tolerating exercise in the heat. It is interesting that there are few heat injuries in sport (note particularly the information available on road racing in the heat) among women. It is apparent that cardiovascular fitness is more important than gender in heat tolerance.

Children in the Heat

Young children are more prone than adults to heat-related injuries (Bar-Or, 1982). The reasons for this are related primarily to the morphological and functional differences between children and adults listed in Table 2.1.

A young child has about 35% to 40% more surface area per kilogram of body weight than a young adult. This results in a significantly greater heat transfer between the skin and the environment through conduction, convection, and radiation. When the air temperature exceeds skin temperature, the child will be at a distinct disadvantage. (The same is true when the air temperature is below skin temperature.)

There are also distinct differences in energy expenditure between children and adults. Walking or running side-by-side, children may expend 20% to 30% more energy per kilogram of body weight than an adult. This means that in

Table 2.1

Morphological and Functional Differences Between Children and Adults and Implications for Thermoregulation

Typical of Children	Effect on Thermoregulation
Greater surface area/mass ratio	Greater rates of heat exchange between skin and environment
Greater energy expenditure during walking and running	Greater production of metabolic heat per kilogram body weight
Lower sweating rate at rest and exercise	Potentially lower capacity for evaporative cooling
Lower cardiac output at a given metabolic level	Lower capacity for heat convection from body core to periphery

Note. From The child athlete and thermoregulation (p. 128) by O. Bar-Or, 1982. In P.V. Komi (Ed.), *Exercise and Sport Biology*. Champaign, IL: Human Kinetics. Reprinted with permission.

both neutral and in hot environments children produce more metabolic heat (Bar-Or et al., 1969; Haymes et al., 1974; Åstrand, 1952).

Sweating rates in children are lower than in adults (Drinkwater et al., 1977; Haymes et al., 1975; Inbar, 1978; Wagner et al., 1972). This difference stems from a lower production of sweat per gland rather than a smaller number of sweat glands (Bar-Or, 1982). Even though sweat losses are not as great as in adults, children do not instinctively drink enough fluid to replenish what is lost during prolonged exercise, and therefore, they are especially prone to dehydration (American Academy of Pediatrics, 1983).

Children do not have as well-developed cardiovascular systems as adults. At a given metabolic rate, the cardiac output of children is lower than that of adults in both neutral and hot environments (Bar-Or et al., 1971; Drinkwater et al., 1977). This means that the child has a somewhat limited ability to bring internal heat to the surface of the body for dissipation to the environment. Despite these disadvantages, children and preadolescents can acclimatize to exercise in the heat—but they do so to a lesser degree than adults (Inbar, 1978; Wagner, Robinson, Tzankoff & Marino, 1972).

The American Academy of Pediatrics (1983) has provided the following guidelines for teachers, coaches, and parents of children exercising in the heat:

1. The intensity of activities that last 30 minutes or more should be reduced whenever relative humidity and air temperature are above critical levels. (see Table 2.2). Information concerning relative humidity may be obtained from a nearby US National Weather Service office or by use of a sling psychrom-

eter (School Health Supplies, Box 409, 300 Lombard Rd, Addison, IL 60101; approximate cost $30) to compare dry bulb and wet bulb temperature levels.

2. At the beginning of a strenuous exercise program or after traveling to a warmer climate, the intensity and duration of exercise should be restrained initially and then gradually increased over a period of 10 to 14 days to accomplish acclimatization to the effects of heat.

3. Before prolonged physical activity, the child should be fully hydrated. During the activity, periodic drinking (e.g., 150 ml of cold tap water each 30 minutes for a child weighing 40 kg) should be enforced.

4. Clothing should be lightweight, limited to one layer of absorbent material in order to facilitate evaporation of sweat and to expose as much skin as possible. Sweat-saturated garments should be replaced by dry ones. Rubberized sweat suits should never be used to produce loss of weight.

GUIDELINES FOR EXERCISE PERFORMANCE IN THE HEAT

Heat Injury

Heat disorders occur when the effector mechanisms are incapable of adjusting body heat loss in relation to heat gain. Table 2.3 gives the causes of most heat injuries and disorders, their symptoms, and some suggested treatments. There is insufficient statistical information to describe the frequency of these disorders, but the

Table 2.2

Weather Guide for Prevention of Heat Illness

Air Temperature	Danger Zone	Critical Zone
70 F	80% RH	100% RH
75 F	70% RH	100% RH
80 F	50% RH	80% RH
85 F	40% RH	68% RH
90 F	30% RH	55% RH
95 F	20% RH	40% RH
100 F	10% RH	30% RH

RH = relative humidity

Note. Data compiled from *The physiological basis of physical education and athletics* (3rd ed.), (p. 475) by E.L. Fox and D.K. Mathews, 1981, Philadelphia: Saunders College Publishing, and *Physiology of exercise: Responses and adaptations* (p. 281), 1978, D.R. Lamb, New York: Macmillan Publishing Co.

Table 2.3

Heat Disorders: Treatment and Prevention

Disorder	Cause	Clinical Features and Diagnosis	Treatment	Prevention
I. Heat cramps	Hard work in heat Heavy and prolonged sweating Inadequate salt intake	Low serum sodium and chloride Muscle twitching, cramps, and spasms in arms, legs, and abdomen—usually after mid-day	Severe case: intravenous administration of 500 ml of normal saline Light case: oral administration of saline Rest in cool environment Salt foods used Delay 24 to 48 hrs before re-entering hot area	Insure acclimatization Provide extra salt at meals Drink saline when working
II. Heat syncope	Peripheral vasodilation and pooling of blood Circulatory instability and loss of vasomotor tone Cerebral hypoxia Hyperventilation Inadequate acclimatization Infection	Weakness and fatigue Hypotension Increased venous compliance Blurred vision Pallor Syncope Elevated skin and deep body temperatures	Place supine and lower head Rest in cool environment Provide oral saline if conscious and resting Keep record of blood pressure, pulse rate, and body temperature	Insure acclimatization Lighten work regimen with sudden rise in environmental temperatures or humidity Avoid maintenance of upright static work conditions Comment: Predisposes to heat stroke

Table 2.3 cont.

Disorder	Cause	Clinical Features and Diagnosis	Treatment	Prevention
III. Water depletion heat exhaustion	Heavy and prolonged sweating Inadequate fluid intake Polyuria or diarrhea	Reduced sweating, but excessive weight loss Elevated skin and deep body temperatures High hematocrit, serum protein, and sodium Dry tongue and mouth Excessive thirst Hyporexia Weak, disconsolate, uncoordinated, and mentally dull Concentrated urine	Bed rest in cool environment Replace fluids by intravenous drip if drinking is impaired, increase fluids to 6 or 8 liters per day Sponge with cool water Provide small quantities of semi-liquid food Keep record of body weight, water and salt intake, and body temperature	Provide adequate water Provide opportunity for intermittent cooling and adequate rest
IV. Salt depletion leading to heat exhaustion	Heavy and prolonged sweating Inadequate acclimatization Vomiting or diarrhea	Headache, dizziness, and fatigue Hyporexia Nausea, vomiting, diarrhea Muscle cramps Syncope High hematocrit and serum protein, but low plasma volume Uremia and hypercalemia Low sodium and chloride in sweat and urine	Bed rest in cool environment Replace fluids and salt by intravenous saline drip if drinking is impaired Provide small quantities of semi-liquid food Keep record of urinary osmolarity or specific gravity, blood urea, and serum sodium or chloride Keep record of body weight, water and salt intake, and body temperature	Provide adequate salt and water; 10 to 15 gms of salt per day may be necessary Provide opportunity for intermittent cooling and adequate rest Insure acclimatization Comment: Develops more slowly (3-5 days) than water depletion heat exhaustion

Table 2.3 cont.

Disorder	Cause	Clinical Features and Diagnosis	Treatment	Prevention
V. Heat hyper-pyrexia lead-ing to heat stroke	Thermoregularity failure of sudden onset	General anhidrosis and dry skin Elevated skin and deep body temperatures frequently over 40.5° C (105° F), may have chills Irrational Muscle flaccidity Involuntary limb movements Seizures and coma Spotty cyanosis and ecchymosis Vomiting and diarrhea, frequently with blood Tachycardia and tachypnea	Lower body temperature to 38.9° C (102° F), within 1 hour, with cold rinse or spray 7.2° C (45° F). Use cool air fan or place in ice water bath. Use alcohol rinse if nothing else available Use suction equipment to clear airway and perform tracheotomy if necessary Inject 25-30 mg chloropromazine every 30 minutes Bed rest in cool environment Keep record of skin and deep body temperatures Treat secondary disorders	Insure acclimatization Adapt activities to environment Screen participants with infection or past history of heat illness
VI. Skin lesions	Constantly wetted Overexposure to sun	Erythematous papulovesicular rash Itchy skin Obstruction of sweat ducts	Maintain shaded, and dry skin Rest in cool environment	Dry skin when possible and keep shaded Examine skin regularly Provide opportunity for intermittent cooling and adequate sweat free periods

Note. From Heat injury and conduct of athletes (p. 50) by E.R. Buskirk and W.C. Grasley, 1968. In *Physiological aspects of sports and physical fitness.* Chicago: Athletic Institute. Reprinted with permission.

most common heat disorders are probably heat syncope and water depletion heat exhaustion.

The major distinction between heat exhaustion, which is fairly common, and heat stroke, which is more rare, is often said to be a dry skin. Although this is not absolutely reliable, it is probably a reasonable field guideline for distinguishing between the two. It is important to be able to do so, because heat stroke is immediately life threatening. To prevent death, the elevated body temperature *must* be lowered as soon as possible. With heat stroke, there is a failure of thermoregulation. That is, the heat loss mechanisms are not even attempting to cool the body. With heat exhaustion, the mechanisms have been hard at work but are inadequate to sufficiently cool the body. Sometimes this happens because the environment is too stressful for the person to adjust to, and sometimes it occurs because the individual is incapable of the necessary responses. Some people are particularly susceptible to heat disorder—for example, those who are not accustomed to the heat, have been ill recently, have circulatory or heart diseases, are obese, are elderly, and are extremely sedentary and suddenly exercise strenuously in the heat. A common denominator here is lack of sufficient cardiovascular fitness to make the physiological adjustments necessary for adequate thermoregulation under unusual circumstances.

Environmental Guidelines

One accepted and useful method of evaluating environmental stress is the wet bulb globe temperature (WBGT) index. This index combines wet bulb temperature (T_{wb}) with dry bulb temperature (T_{db}) and radiant temperature from the environment. Radiant heat is measured with the globe thermometer mentioned earlier (T_g).

$$WBGT = 0.7\ T_{wb} + 0.2\ T_g + 0.1\ T_{db}$$

Because relative humidity is the most important environmental factor, it is given more weight in the WBGT index. Under conditions where radiant heat is not an important factor, T_g is omitted, and the constant for T_{db} becomes 0.3. Table 2.4 gives the recommended Occupational Safety and Health Association guidelines for heat stress threshold values for WBGT.

The American College of Sports Medicine (1984) has published a position stand on the "Prevention of thermal injuries during distance running." The College recommends that summer distance races be conducted before 8 a.m. and after 6 p.m. to minimize solar radiation and that races be rescheduled or delayed when WBGT exceeds 28° C (82° F). The statement places the onus of responsibility on race sponsors (1) to educate participants regarding thermal injury, susceptibility and prevention, (2) to provide water before the race and every 2 to 3 km during the

Table 2.4

Recommendation of OSHA Committee for Heat Stress—
Threshold Values for WBGT C (F)

Work Load	Low Air Velocity <1.53 m•sec⁻¹ (300 fpm)	High Air Velocity >1.53 m•sec⁻¹ (300 fpm)
Light:		
< 200 kcal•h⁻¹	30.0 (86)	32.2 (90)
Moderate:		
201-300 kcal•h⁻¹	27.8 (82)	30.6 (87)
Heavy:		
> 300 kcal•h⁻¹	26.1 (79)	28.9 (84)

Note. From Prevention of heat injuries (p. 144) by E.M. Haymes and E.R. Buskirk, 1980. In G.A. Stull (Ed.) *Encyclopedia of physical education, fitness, and sports: Training, environment, nutrition, and fitness.* Salt Lake City: Brighton Publishing Co. Reprinted with permission.

race, and (3) to provide adequate medical care. The complete statement is contained in Appendix B.

The Importance of Fluid Replacement

Water is the most abundant constituent in the human body, and it may be the most valuable as well. Water constitutes about 63% of the body weight in men and about 52% in women. About half of this water is within the cells (intracellular water), where it acts as an active support medium for metabolic reactions. The extracellular compartment provides about 22% of the body weight and serves as the major transportation system for respiratory gases, cellular substrates and by-products, and metabolic heat. Water is the basis of the circulatory system.

The ability to perform endurance exercise is directly related to the capacity of the circulatory system to transport oxygen to the working muscles. Because there is not sufficient blood volume to fill the entire circulatory system all at once, blood is distributed throughout the body on the basis of need. During rest blood flows freely to the internal organs and to the skin for heat dissipation (if necessary), but relatively little flows to the muscles. During strenuous and prolonged exertion, however, this blood flow pattern is altered significantly from the inactive tissues to the active tissues. Now it is essential to circulate blood to the contracting muscles. The capacity to do that depends on the volume of blood available for distribution and the ability to divert a large part of that volume to the muscles (Costill, 1980). Anything that interferes with this function will seriously affect an athlete's performance.

A significant decline in body water will result in a corresponding decline in plasma volume and consequently of blood volume. Not only will blood flow to the muscles be impaired, but so will the ability to dissipate internal body heat via vasodilatation of the subcutaneous vessels. When even as much as 2% of the body weight has been lost from sweating, performance will be negatively affected. Eventually, the important thermoregulatory function of sweating will decline and fail. When that happens, water-depletion heat exhaustion has occurred, and the athlete will collapse.

Dehydration

Dehydration equivalent to even 2% of body weight can noticeably impair performance by compromising the circulatory and thermoregulatory functions (Pitts, Johnson, & Consolazio, 1944; Adolph, 1947; Åstrand and Saltin, 1964; Saltin, 1964). The decline in performance is caused by (a) the reduction in blood volume and consequently in maximal cardiac output and peripheral circulation; (b) the disturbance in central nervous system control of the sweat glands and/or peripheral vasculature from thermal or osmolar effects on the hypothalamus; (c) a reduction in the capacity of the sweat glands to secrete sweat (sweat gland fatigue); and (d) suppressed cellular function leading to a reduction in anaerobic capacity (for more extensive references, see Herbert, 1980).

With increasing levels of dehydration, there are striking declines in endurance performance and elevations in heart rate and body core temperature. It is obvious that to prevent this, the exercise participant must replace the water that is lost via sweating. What is not quite so obvious is the best method to do this. The ideal situation would be not only to replace the fluid lost but to duplicate its composition. Let's examine what is lost in sweat in more detail.

Sweat Composition

Sweat is a filtrate of blood plasma and as such contains many of the same substances. As described earlier, however, the sweat glands are capable of conserving certain substances. Consequently, sweat is more dilute than the other fluids of the body. See Table 2.5 for a comparison of the concentrations of sodium and chloride in sweat and blood plasma. Because sweat has approximately one third of the concentration of Na^+ and Cl^- as plasma, sweat is hypotonic to plasma.

The most abundant minerals in sweat are sodium and chloride. These electrolytes are located in the extracellular fluid compartment and are primarily responsible for maintaining the water content of that compartment. This con-

Table 2.5

Electrolyte (mEq – L^{-1}) Concentration of Plasma and Sweat

	Sodium	Chloride	Potassium	Magnesium	Total
Plasma	140	100	4	1.5	245.5
Sweat	40-60	30-50	5-5	1.5-5	75.5-120

Note. From Fluids for athletic performance: Why and what you should drink during prolonged exercise (p. 132) by D. Costill, 1980. In E.J. Burke (Ed.), *Toward an understanding of human performance* (2nd ed.). New York: Movement Publications. Reprinted with permission.

trol requires a steady relationship between the concentration (number) of ions, and significant electrolyte loss can disrupt this relationship. When that occurs, body water must be redistributed to maintain the proper water-ion relationship (Costill, 1980). However, when sweat is lost, far more water is lost than electrolytes, leaving the remaining electrolytes in the body water more concentrated. Therefore, as far as the cells are concerned, there is an excess rather than a depletion of electrolytes. The point of all this is that *it is far more important to replace the water than the electrolytes*. In fact, although this is not an absolutely closed question, it is probably not important to replace sweat electrolytes *during* an athletic event. The primary need is *fluid* replacement.

Potassium loss in sweat has been emphasized by the popular press. Contrary to the opinions offered by various health food advocates, potassium loss in sweat is low. Potassium is located primarily in the intracellular fluid compartment and is found only in low concentration in the extracellular fluid space from which most of the sweat comes. The actual loss in sweat is about 0.01 oz of potassium per quart of sweat (Senay, 1979). Even with low dietary potassium intake and high potassium losses in sweat, little change in total body potassium (less than 2%) has been reported (Costill, 1980). Therefore, potassium loss in sweat is probably of little consequence, and one need not be concerned about replacing it during exercise.

There are at least three benefits to ingesting fluids during exercise when significant sweat losses occur: First, by minimizing the degree of dehydration that would occur from prolonged sweating, the stress placed on the circulatory system is significantly reduced. Consequently, more blood is available to transport metabolic substrates and by-products and to transfer heat to the body's shell. Second, by taking fluids during exercise, the threat of overheating is significantly reduced. A third possible benefit is that fluid replacement offers an opportunity to supplement or replace the metabolic substrate (carbohydrate) consumed during exercise. This third benefit may, however, prove detrimental to the first two. Nonetheless, many people advocate glucose ingestion during exercise.

Glucose Ingestion During Prolonged Exercise

When the duration of exercise exceeds several hours, the liver releases glucose into the blood from its glycogen store for use by the active tissues. Eventually, the liver will become depleted of glycogen and the blood glucose level will drop below that desired to maintain the working cells. Readers are probably familiar with the expression "hitting the wall" that is used by marathon runners (cyclists use the expression "getting the bonks"). When this occurs, performance deteriorates considerably, and the race is usually abandoned.

Blood glucose levels can be maintained if glucose is absorbed from the small intestine. A fluid replacement substance that contains carbohydrates is often prescribed to resupply the glycogen and glucose used by the working tissues.

This solution has a serious drawback when exercising in the heat, however. It is clear that the most important substance to replace during exercise in the heat is water. Replacing other substances such as sodium, chloride, potassium, magnesium, and calcium—is of minimal importance. However, the amount of water replaced by consuming fluids during exercise depends on how quickly the drink leaves the stomach. Several factors can affect the rate of gastric emptying—the volume consumed, the temperature of the fluid, and the sugar content. The most important factor, however, is the concentration of sugar (glucose) in the solution. All sugars (including honey and fructose) significantly retard the rate at which solutions leave the stomach. Thus, consuming a sugar solution is a poor method of replacing the body water lost as sweat. (See Costill & Saltin, 1974; Coyle, Costill, Fink, & Hoopes, 1978; Costill & Sparks, 1973). As a result of several studies on this topic the best recommendation is to drink water when that is the substance that is most important to replace under the exercise and environmental circumstances. When it is imperative to replace the glucose lost during exercise, the best replacement solution is a mild concentration of carbohydrate such as 2.0 to 2.5 gm of glucose per 100 ml of water (Costill, 1980; "Prevention of Thermal Injury," 1984).

Thirst

Under normal environmental conditions, the thirst mechanism is usually adequate to maintain water balance. The urge to drink is mediated by the hypothalamus, which is responsive to increased body fluid osmolarity (concentration) with water depletion (Åstrand and Rodahl, 1977). Because more water than body salts are lost through sweating, blood osmolarity increases. If sufficient water is drunk to replace losses the osmolarity is reduced, and water balance is reestablished. However, when individuals sweat profusely during exercise, they invariably fail to voluntarily replace their losses (Adolph, 1947). This is called voluntary dehydration, and it has been noted by many investigators. For example, marathon runners drink so sparingly that weight deficits exceeding 5% of body weight are common (Pugh, Corbett, & Johnson,

(1967). Generally, coaches should teach athletes that thirst is not an adequate indicator of the need for water and that they should maintain a proper state of hydration during participation.

Subjects allowed ad libitum water intake during a prolonged march had lower heart rates, lower rectal temperatures, and fewer dropouts than subjects not receiving any water (Strydom, Wyndham, van Graan, Holdsworth, & Morrison, 1966). However, the thirst mechanism was inadequate to prevent dehydration, and the ad libitum water drinkers had a water deficit of 2.9% at the end of the march. Other studies have verified that most sport competitors undergo voluntary dehydration between 2% and 7% of their body weight, and the more successful competitors usually incur the largest water losses. Competitors who consume the largest amounts of water usually show the least elevation in rectal temperatures (Wyndham and Strydom, 1969).

In studies comparing ad libitum water consumption and forced replacement of sweat losses it is clear that the latter procedure is the least stressful. With forced ingestion of fluids (i.e., fluid ingestion is matched with sweat losses), subjects showed lower rectal temperatures, better heat dissipation, and sometimes lower heart rates (Pitts, et al., 1944; Dill, Yousef, & Nelson, 1973; Costill, Kammer, & Fisher, 1970).

Practical Suggestions Regarding Fluid Replacement During Exercise In the Heat

Optimal physical performance is not possible if one becomes dehydrated. It is therefore extremely important that fluids be taken during exercise when large amounts of sweat are lost. Hyperhydration (taking ample water *before* performance) has been found to aid performance and was associated with significantly lower rectal temperatures, lower heart rates, higher sweat rates, and longer treadmill performance times (Herbert, 1980).

Costill (1980) has provided some guidelines for fluid replacement during hot weather exercise. He suggests that the drink be hypotonic, low in sugar concentration (less than 2.5 gm per 100 ml of water), cold (roughly 45° to 55° F or 8° to 13° C), consumed in volumes ranging from 100 to 400 ml (3 to 10 oz), and of palatable taste. He further suggests that 400 to 600 ml (13.5 to 20 oz) of water be consumed 30 minutes before the competition, and 100 to 200 ml (3 to 6.5 oz) be consumed during activity. For electrolyte replacement, Costill suggests modest salting of foods *after* the event. For any event exceeding 50 or 60 minutes, fluid replacement is essential. Keeping a record of early morning body weight from day to day is a good method of detecting dehydration.

ACCLIMATIZATION

It has long been recognized that the human can gradually adjust to hot climates. With acclimatization, marked decreases are found in heart rate and skin and body core temperatures as shown in Figure 2.5. In addition, the dizziness, weakness, and nausea that often occur with exertion in the heat disappear, and exercise capacity improves dramatically. Other adaptive responses include an increase in sweating rate, an earlier onset of sweating (i.e., at a lower body temperature), and a more complete and even distribution of sweat over the

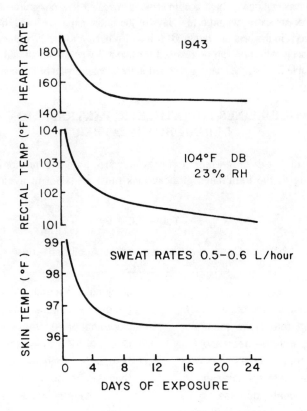

Figure 2.5 Changes in heart rate, skin and core temperatures with heat acclimatization.

Note. From Historical perspectives of adaptation to heat (p. 17) by S.M. Horvath, 1981. In S.M. Horvath and M.K. Yousef (Eds.) *Environmental physiology: Aging, heat, and altitude.* New York: Elsevier/North Holland. Reprinted with permission.

skin. The increased economy of physiological responses to the heat is also shown by the decrease in electrolytes in the sweat and the improved maintenance of body fluid volume and composition. It is likely that the adrenal hormone, aldosterone, plays a major role in this adaptation. Aldosterone is known to conserve sodium, the major electrolyte in sweat. With full acclimatization there is enhanced tissue conductance in the periphery. This is accomplished by increased perfusion of the cutaneous interstitial space, which results in an increase in plasma volume (Frisancho, 1979, p. 23). Apparently, the ability to dissipate body heat is enhanced by the progressive physiological adjustments that occur with gradual acclimatization as shown in Figure 2.6.

Early investigations of heat acclimatization revealed that physiological adaptations can occur soon—within a few days of the initial exposure—and that regular work periods in the heat are required. It has also been reasonably well established that heat acclimatization can be retained for about 3 weeks without additional exposure. Table 2.6 lists the changes reported in the literature with heat acclimatization.

GUIDELINES FOR ATHLETIC PARTICIPATION DURING HOT WEATHER

Exercise in hot-dry, hot-humid, or even warm-humid conditions can be devastating to the uninitiated. Precautions must be taken to avoid serious

Table 2.6

Changes Observed Consequent to Acclimatization

Heart rate—decrease	Subjective discomfort—decrease
Stroke volume—increase	Fatigue—decrease
Core temperature—decrease	Coordination—increase
Skin temperature—decrease	Capacity for work—increase
Sweat output—increase	Mental disturbances—decrease
Evaporated sweat—increase	Syncopal responses—decrease
Onset of sweat—increase	Extracellular fluid volume—
Wetted body surface—increase	increase
Skin and core temperature at onset—	Plasma volume—increase
decrease	Nausea—decrease
NaCl in sweat—decrease	Vomiting—decrease
Work output—increase	

Note. Adapted from Historical Perspectives of Adaptation to Heat (p. 16) by S.M. Horvath, 1981. In S.M. Horvath and M.K. Yousef (Eds.) Environmental physiology: Aging, heat, and altitude. New York: Elsevier/North Holland, Inc.

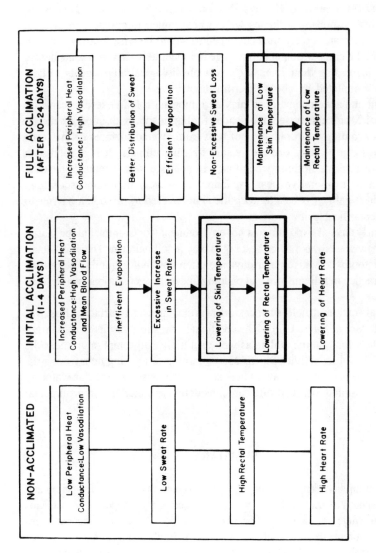

Figure 2.6 Schemata for the mechanisms of acclimatization to heat stress.

Note. From Human adaptation: A functional interpretation (p. 24) by A.R. Frisancho, 1979, St. Louis: C.V. Mosby Co. Reprinted with permission.

medical problems. Awareness of a few simple principles may lead to successful performance as well as safety. For example, becoming gradually accustomed to participation in hot or warm climates considerably reduces the physiological strain associated with sudden exposure.

The best way to become acclimatized to hot environments is to gradually expose yourself over 4 to 10 days. Mild to moderate exercise enhances the physiological responses. Athletes who are scheduled to compete in a warm or hot climate that they are unaccustomed to would be wise to arrive several days before the competition and to engage in moderately easy workouts before gradually increasing their intensity. Most physiological adjustments to heat should be completed by about the fifth day.

Frequent and adequate *rest* can play an important role in exercise capacity in the heat. Momentarily seeking shade, finding a spot with good air movement, and avoiding the reradiation of heat from ground surfaces or the walls of buildings can prolong one's exposure to a hot climate. It is a good idea to loosen or remove clothing when that will enhance loss of internal heat via convection or evaporative heat exchange. However, in instances of high radiative heat gain, it is best to keep the skin covered to provide a barrier to environmental heat gain.

In the early days of exposure to a hot environment (for example, at the beginning of a new season), it may be best not to play in full uniform. This is especially true for football. Midsummer days are often hot and/or humid. Beginning football practice in full uniform and padding under these conditions has resulted in deaths.

Artificial track and field surfaces are warmer than turf surfaces (Buskirk, Loomis, & McLaughlin, 1971). The additional heat stress results from a larger radiative heat load on the athlete as well as a higher air temperature near the surface. Scheduling activity for the early morning or evening hours when the solar load is less severe can avoid heat stress problems. The regular watering of both natural and artificial turf can considerably reduce the environmental heat load.

SUMMARY

The relationship between physiology effector mechanisms for heat dissipation and physical avenues of heat exchange was emphasized in this chapter. Each effector mechanism, while leading to significant body heat loss, also causes secondary consequences that must be countered in some way. Vasodilatation, for example, leads to significant changes in blood flow that require an increase in cardiac output. Under some conditions, SV may decrease considerably. If $\dot{Q}$ cannot be maintained at a sufficient level, syncope may occur.

While evaporation of sweat from the body surface is an important means for heat loss, a number of consequences occur that could seriously affect performance. Because sweat is hypotonic to body fluids, water replacement is essential to maintain blood volume with prolonged or profuse sweating. The kidney vigorously protects water balance. With high sweating rates, ADH is elevated, and acts on the renal tubule to conserve body water. Aldosterone mediates the reabsorption of sodium which plays a significant role in maintaining the extracellular fluid compartment.

In a thermally neutral environment, no thermoregulatory effect is required. With environmental heat stress, however, considerable thermoregulatory effort is required. The ability to tolerate strenuous exercise in the heat is largely a matter of cardiovascular fitness. The endurance trained individual is able to maintain an adequate blood flow to active muscles as well as skin surfaces, and consequently, can cool the body while continuing to exercise.

There are some differences in how men and women respond to heat stress. While cardiovascularly fit women are as heat tolerant as men, they generally sweat less, and have higher heart rates and skin temperatures. Children are not as heat tolerant as adults.

There are several forms of heat injury. Heat stroke can be life threatening. The best means of prevention is having an understanding of environmental guidelines for exposure to heat as provided by OSHA and ACSM.

The most important factor in performance in the heat is fluid replacement. If body water is allowed to decline significantly, blood flow to muscles and skin surfaces will be impaired, sweating will decline, and body temperature regulation may fail. Although body electrolytes are lost in sweat, electrolyte replacement should occur *following* exercise rather than *during* exercise. Glucose containing drinks retard the absorption of water from the gastrointestinal tract. When it is imperative to replace carbohydrate substrate during prolonged exercise, only weak glucose solutions should be used or water depletion may result.

Gradual acclimatization to heat results in significant changes in physiological response. Athletes should be sure they are adequately acclimatized before competing in the heat.

3

Cold Environments and Human Performance

Exercise in a cold environment seems to be better tolerated than exercise in a warm environment. In this chapter we will examine why heat loss is facilitated in the cold and discuss the defense mechanisms used by humans to prevent heat loss from becoming excessive. Next we will examine whether the physiological responses to exercise are altered by a cold environment. We will examine the roles played by body fat, clothing, and wind in altering the rate of heat loss. Finally we will discuss the effects of cold on athletic performance. The following questions will be discussed:

- Are the responses to exercise in cold air the same as those seen in cold water?
- Is a water environment more dangerous than cold air?
- What factors influence our responses to the cold?
- Are women better able to prevent heat loss than men?
- Does the level of physical fitness affect the responses to exercise in the cold?
- Can humans adapt to the cold after prolonged exposure?
- What happens when the defense mechanisms fail?
- How do you recognize the symptoms of hypothermia and frostbite?
- Does cold enhance or inhibit performance?

THERMAL BALANCE IN THE COLD

How does a person respond to the cold? There have been fewer studies of the responses to cold than to warm environments. One reason for less research in this area is that a true cold environment may not exist, even though the ambient temperature is below the thermally neutral range (23° C to 31° C). This is because the microclimate next to the skin is maintained at a higher temperature by extra layers of clothing. For example, the downhill skier may maintain his or her skin temperature 25° C or more above the ambient temperature by wearing several layers of clothing, including long underwear and a down parka. In this case, the skier may not feel cold until environmental conditions exceed the insulative capacity of the clothing, which could occur if the ambient temperature decreased, wind velocity increased, and/or the clothing became wet.

Exposure to a cold environment can lead to excessive heat loss. Thermal balance in a cold environment can be expressed by the equation:

$$M \pm W - E \pm R \pm C \pm K = S$$

In the cold, both R and C will be negative, because ambient temperature is below skin temperature. If heat is lost at a faster rate than it is produced, then S (stored body heat) will be negative. When S is negative, body tissues are cooling and the mean body temperature (T_b) is decreasing. If S = 0, then the rate of heat production balances the rate of heat loss. Metabolic heat production (M) can be increased by increasing $\dot{V}O_2$. Physical work (W) is considered to be zero when a person is resting. During exercise W can easily be calculated on a cycle ergometer.

Evaporative heat loss is not as large in the cold as in hot environments. Evaporation occurs through both the skin (E_{sw}) and through the respiratory tract (E_{res}). The equations for calculating both the combined evaporative heat loss (E) as well as R, K, C, and M are in the first chapter. Evaporative heat loss through the respiratory tract depends on the rate of ventilation and the vapor pressure gradient between the exhaled air and the environment. Because the relative humidity and temperature of exhaled air are 100% and 37° C, respectively, the vapor pressure in the lungs will remain constant at 47 torr while the ambient vapor pressure will decrease as temperature decreases. This means that the vapor pressure gradient will increase in the cold, and more heat will be lost through E_{res} than in warmer environments. The increase in heat loss through respiration is more than counterbalanced by reduced evaporation from the skin. Evaporative heat loss through the skin depends on the rate of sweating, the vapor pressure gradient between the skin and air, the permeation of moisture through the clothing, and the air velocity. Because sweating is reduced in the cold, E_{sw} is not as large as in hot environments.

Radiation and convection are more important sources of heat loss in the cold than in warmer environments. Heat loss through radiation occurs when skin temperature (or clothing temperature) is above the temperature of the environmental surroundings. The temperature gradient between the skin and surroundings is the major factor that determines the amount of heat lost. Convec-

Table 3.1

Convective Heat Loss Coefficients

Activity	h_c (W/m² × C)
Standing	3.2
Sitting	4.0
Bicycle ergometer—50 rpm	5.4
Treadmill walking—3 mph	7.2
Free walking—3 mph	9.0
Resting in water	230
Swimming—0.5 m·s⁻¹	580

Data compiled from Nadel, Holmer, Bergh, Åstrand, & Stolwijk (1974). "Energy exchanges of swimming man," *Journal of Applied Physiology*, **36**, 465-471, and Nishi & Gagge (1970), "Direct evaluation of convective heat transfer coefficient by naphthalene sublimation," *Journal of Applied Physiology*, **29**, 830-838.

tive heat loss occurs when air is warmed by contact with the warm body. Both the temperature gradient between T_{sk} and T_a and the air velocity are important factors in determining convective heat loss. The convective heat loss coefficients (h_c) for several different activities are presented in Table 3.1. Some heat loss also occurs through the respiratory tract as the air is warmed during inhalation. Convective heat loss through the respiratory tract can be calculated as follows:

$$C_{res} = .0014 \ M \ (35 - T_a).$$

In water, heat loss through conduction must also be considered. Water is an excellent conductor of heat, more than 20 times that of air. Heat loss through conduction depends on the temperature gradient between the skin and water. Although heat is conducted directly from the skin to the water, most of the heat loss in a water environment is removed by convection, because warm water moves away from the body and is replaced by colder water. Heat loss is increased in moving water. The calculated h_c during swimming is more than twice that during rest in still water, but h_c remains constant as the velocity of swimming increases (Nadel, Holmer, Bergh, Åstrand, & Stolwijk, 1974).

Insulation is the reciprocal of heat conduction. The total insulation (I_{tot}) is the sum of the air insulation, clothing insulation, and tissue insulation:

$I_{tot} = I_a + I_{cl} + I_t$
  where I_a = air insulation
  I_{cl} = clothing insulation
  I_t = tissue insulation

Air insulation is determined by the velocity of air movement and is greatest when the air is still. Clothing insulation is determined by the type of fabric, the thickness of the clothing, and whether the fabric is wet (see Table 3.2). It is advantageous to layer clothing in cold environments, because air trapped between layers increases insulation. Most fabrics are poor insulators when they are wet. This has led to the design of special clothing that can be worn as an outer garment during wet weather or water immersion. For example, scuba divers and surfers wear neoprene wet suits in cold water. We will discuss factors that influence tissue insulation in the next section.

Assume that a person weighing 70 kg is resting in a room with an air temperature of 15° C (60° F). The normal resting metabolic rate (M) for this person would be approximately 72 watts. If the heat loss through R and C and E was 118 watts, heat loss would exceed heat gain by 46 watts. The amount of heat lost from storage (S) can be estimated from the change in mean body temperature (dT_b/dt):

$S = 0.97$ m (dT_b/dt)
  where $T_b = 0.67 T_{re} + 0.33 T_{sk}$,
  0.97 = specific heat of the body in watts/kg ° C,
  m = body weight in kg.

In this example, dT_b/dt would equal $46/(0.97 \times 70)$, or 0.64° C. In other words, the body is cooling at a rate of 0.64° C every hour.

PHYSIOLOGICAL RESPONSES TO A COLD ENVIRONMENT

Are there any mechanisms that can prevent or at least reduce the rate of heat loss? There are two primary physiological responses used by humans to defend against a cold environment: increased metabolic rate and increased tissue insulation. Increases in metabolic rate can be involuntary (thermogenesis) or voluntary (increased physical activity). Tissue insulation is increased by constricting blood vessels in the superficial tissues. Humans also use behavioral responses such as adding clothing and seeking a warm shelter to combat a cold environment.

Thermogenesis

Thermogenesis in the cold is primarily due to shivering—the involuntary contraction of superficial muscle fibers. Because the muscle contractions do not

Table 3.2

Insulation of Clothing Materials

Clothing	I_{cl} (clo)
Down, goose—2.1 cm loft	1.64
Wool—1.9 cm loft	1.52
Polyester (Dacron)—1.7 cm loft	1.20
Polyolefin—1.2 cm loft	1.14
Nylon cross-country ski racing uniform with polyolefin underwear	1.60
Anorak, wool jersey, shirt, string vest and jeans	2.49
Standard arctic clothing	4.90
Standard arctic clothing with nylon outer garment	5.30

Data compiled from Haymes, Dickinson, Malville, & Ross (1982), "Effects of wind on thermal and metabolic responses to exercise in the cold," *Medicine and Science in Sports and Exercise,* **14**, 41-45; Horvath (1948), "Reactions of men exposed to cold and wind," *American Journal of Physiology,* **152**, 242-249; Kaufman, Bothe, & Meyer (1982), "Thermal insulating capabilities and outdoor clothing materials," *Science,* **215**, 690-691; Pugh (1966), "Clothing insulation and accidental hypothermia in youth," *Nature,* **209**, 1281-1286.

produce any work, the energy released is converted to heat. Shivering thermogenesis can increase resting metabolism approximately threefold or 3 METS. (One MET is the equivalent of the resting metabolic rate.) In the example of a person resting in a cold environment, heat balance could be achieved by shivering thermogenesis if the metabolic rate increased 60% to 1.6 METS. Another form of thermogenesis, nonshivering thermogenesis, exists in rodents and the newborn of many species. It may also exist in adult humans, but it seems to be of limited usefulness. Nonshivering thermogenesis is due to increased metabolism in brown adipose tissue. When the fat (triglyceride) is mobilized, the fatty acids are metabolized in the adipose tissue and only glycerol is released into the blood. Norepinephrine is thought to be the stimulus for nonshivering thermogenesis.

Peripheral Vasoconstriction

Before metabolism increases, however, the body usually responds to the cold by constricting blood vessels. With the exception of the head, constriction of superficial blood vessels occurs in most areas of the body when the body is cooled. Shunting of blood flow into the deeper blood vessels effectively increases tissue insulation. The rate of heat loss decreases as tissue thickness increases (see Figure 3.1). When blood flow is shunted away from the skin, the superficial tissues cool and the temperature gradient between the skin and core increases. Tissue insulation can be calculated using the following equation:

$$I_t = (T_c - T_{sk})/(E_{sk} + R + C)$$

Constriction of the cutaneous blood vessels is controlled by the sympathetic nerves. Cold may also have a direct effect on blood vessels, causing them to constrict.

Because vasoconstriction reduces the amount of blood in the superficial vessels, blood flow increases in the deep veins during cooling. Shunting of the blood to the deep veins helps conserve body heat. Deep veins in the extremities are parallel and adjacent to the arteries. Arterial blood flowing away from the trunk will be warmer than the blood returning to the heart in the veins. Heat will flow from the arterial blood to the cooler venous blood, which will warm as it moves from the distal to proximal end of the extremity (see Figure 3.2). This is known as the countercurrent heat exchange mechanism. The importance of this mechanism in conserving body heat in humans is debatable.

Because blood is shunted to the deeper regions of the body, venous return is enhanced. Stroke volume increases and heart rate decreases so that cardiac output remains constant. When shivering occurs and $\dot{V}O_2$ increases, more oxygen must be supplied to the muscles. Both increases in cardiac output and extraction of oxygen from the blood have been observed during shivering ther-

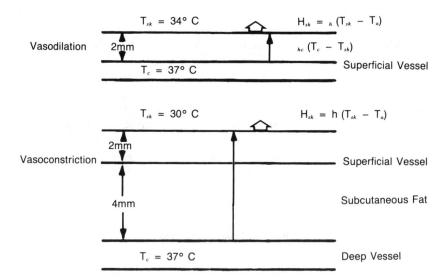

Figure 3.1. Vasodilation and vasoconstriction.

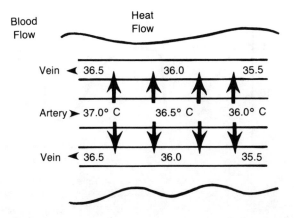

Figure 3.2. Counter current heat exchange.

mogenesis (Raven, Niki, Dahms, & Horvath, 1970). The increased cardiac output was due to both an increase in stroke volume and a slight elevation in heart rate.

Cold Vasodilation

Cold exposure also produces a vasodilation in the extremities. Cold vasodilation was first described by Lewis (1930). When the skin temperature falls below 10° C, blood flow increases to the extremity for a short time before it decreases again (see Figure 3.3). This alternating vasodilation and vasoconstriction is known as the hunting reflex. The increase in blood flow is believed to be due to a relaxation of the arteriovenous anastomoses that shunt the blood to the superficial veins. Arterioles may not respond to sympathetic stimulation when they cool below 10° C (Keatinge, 1969). It has been suggested that cold vasodilation is beneficial in preventing frostbite by warming the tissues. However, heat loss increases from the regions of the body where cold vasodilation occurs. It is debatable whether cold vasodilation serves any purpose.

Thermoregulation in the Cold

Because the superficial blood vessels in the head do not constrict in the cold, the head is an important source of heat loss. It has been estimated that 25% of the total heat lost in a cold environment is from the head (Froese & Burton, 1957). Blood that passes through the superficial vessels in the face enters the brain through the ophthalmic vein. Because heat is lost from the blood in the superficial vessels, the venous blood will be cooler than the arterial blood.

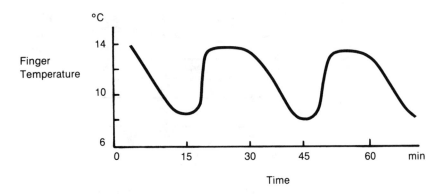

Figure 3.3 Cold vasodilation.

Note. Adapted from *Survival in cold water*, (p. 40) by W.R. Keatinge, 1969, Oxford: Blackwell Scientific Publications Ltd. Adapted with permission.

Cabanac and Caputa (1979) suggested that passage of cooler blood from the face may cool the brain and stimulate vasoconstriction.

Both peripheral and central thermoreceptors appear to have a role in regulating body temperature in cold environments. Peripheral vasoconstriction occurs first, and tissue insulation is maximal before shivering begins. Shivering thermogenesis is stimulated by decreases in skin and core temperature. Cooling of the spinal cord results in shivering thermogenesis and vasoconstriction in some animal species. It seems that the thermoregulatory center in the hypothalamus uses inputs from many thermoreceptors in regulating body temperature in a cold environment. If the core temperature is elevated, the threshold skin temperature at which shivering is stimulated will be reduced. Cabanac (1975) suggested that skin temperature plays a more important role in small animals, because the surface area to mass ratio is larger and heat is lost more rapidly than in large animals. In humans, core temperature is more important than skin temperature because of the relatively large body weight and small surface area to mass ratio.

Cold Diuresis

The volume of urine excreted increases during cold exposure. Increased urine formation is due to a decrease in tubular reabsorption of water in the kidneys rather than an increase in glomerular filtration (Bader, Eliot, & Bass, 1952). In the kidneys, the amount of water reabsorbed into the blood is primarily controlled by the antidiuretic hormone (ADH) secreted by the posterior pituitary. It appears that ADH secretion is reduced during cold exposure. An increase in venous return due to peripheral vasoconstriction is thought to stimulate volume receptors located in the left atrium of the heart. These receptors, in turn, inhibit the secretion of ADH from the posterior pituitary. Cold diuresis is usually accompanied by hemoconcentration, an increase in the blood hematocrit (Adolph & Molnar, 1946; Rochelle & Horvath, 1978). However, the decrease in plasma volume tends to be greater than the increase in urine volume.

EXERCISE RESPONSES

Core Temperature

During exercise the body heat increases because only a fraction of the energy produced (not more than 25%) is used for mechanical work. Most of the energy (more than 75%) is converted to heat, which elevates core temperature. The increase in core temperature occurs during the first 30 to 40 minutes of exercise. However, in a cold climate the final core temperature is lower than in a neutral environment (see Figure 3.4). At low exercise intensities, core temperature cannot be maintained in the cold but will fall after 1 hour of exercise (Andersen, Hart, Hammel, & Sabean, 1963; Stromme, Andersen, & Elsner, 1963). During moderate and heavy exercise, sufficient heat is generated to maintain core temperature.

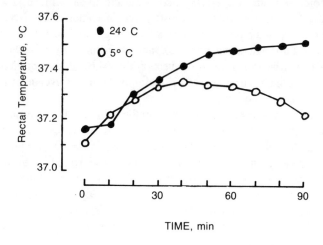

Figure 3.4. Rectal temperature during light exercise (50 w) in neutral and cold environments.

Thermogenesis

The amount of heat produced is insufficient to maintain heat balance at low exercise intensities. The metabolic heat production of subjects in Figure 3.4 was less than the rate of heat loss. Because heat loss exceeds heat gain, body heat content decreases and body temperature falls. The person begins shivering to elevate the metabolic rate. Shivering thermogenesis is stimulated by the decline in skin and core temperatures (Hong & Nadel, 1979; Nielsen, 1976). Shivering thermogenesis seems to occur below a skin temperature threshold during exercise in the cold. Below this threshold, the increase in metabolism is inversely proportional to core temperature. During rewarming, shivering persists during exercise until skin temperatures reach the threshold, even when core temperature is below normal.

Peripheral Vasoconstriction

Some vasoconstriction occurs during exercise in the cold, but not to the same extent as during rest. The reasons for reduced vasoconstriction during exercise are twofold: a need to maintain adequate blood flow to the active skeletal muscles and the increase in core temperature during exercise. Because blood temperature increases during exercise, warm blood flowing through the brain will stimulate the central thermoreceptors for heat loss. Cold receptors located in the skin will simultaneously signal the thermoregulatory center to conserve heat. The result is conflicting stimuli and a reduction in sympathetic vasoconstrictor activity. Although skin temperature declines during exercise in the cold, skin areas overlying active muscle tissue will be at a higher temperature during exercise than at rest. Tissue insulation will also be reduced because of increased blood flow to the skin during exercise. This allows more heat to be lost through convection and evaporation during exercise than at rest. More heat will be lost through convection than through evaporation during exercise in a cold environment. Convection is the major avenue of heat loss during exercise in the cold.

Heart rates are lower during exercise in the cold than in a neutral environment (see Figure 3.5). Peripheral vasoconstriction increases venous return to the heart in the cold, which increases stroke volume compared with the same exercise intensity in a neutral environment. The stimulus for increased vasoconstriction in the cold could be the flushing of cold blood from the periphery through the brain (Cabanac and Caputa, 1979) or cooling of the skin thermoreceptors. Vasoconstriction increases resistance to blood flow and elevates blood pressure. The decrease in heart rate is thought to be due to increased blood pressure, which stimulates baroreceptors located in the aorta and carotid sinus and reflexly slows the heart.

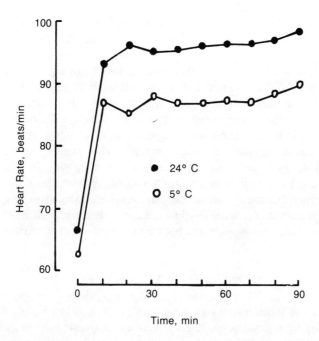

Figure 3.5. Heart rates during light exercise (50 w) in neutral and cold environments.

Substrate Utilization

ATP is the immediate energy source used by muscles during shivering, and free fatty acids are believed to be the main substrate for ATP production (Cabanac, 1975). Increased free fatty acid mobilization has been observed during rest and light exercise when both skin and core temperatures are lowered by cooling (Hurley & Haymes, 1982). Increased fat utilization during exercise in the cold is suggested by a decrease in the respiratory exchange ratio (Hurley & Haymes, 1982; Riggs, Johnson, Kilgour, & Konopka, 1983) and decrease in the muscle triglyceride content (Fink, Costill, & Van Handel, 1975). However, free fatty acid mobilization does not increase at moderate exercise intensities in the cold (Galbo, et al., 1979).

Sympathetic nerve activity is thought to be responsible for the increase in fat mobilization and utilization in the cold. The adrenal medulla releases epinephrine and norepinephrine in response to sympathetic stimulation. Plasma norepinephrine levels increase when either the skin or core temperature is lowered, with the largest increase seen when both skin and core temperatures are reduced (Bergh, Hartley, Landsberg, & Ekblom, 1979). During moderate exercise in the cold, core temperature does not normally decrease. When only skin temperatures are reduced, less norepinephrine is available to mobilize free fatty acids. This may explain why increased fat mobilization has only been observed during light exercise when both core and skin temperatures are reduced.

Several studies have reported increased fat loss following 1 to 2 weeks of exercise in a cold environment (O'Hara, Allen, & Shephard, 1977a & b; O'Hara, Allen, Shephard, & Allen, 1979). The amount of weight lost was greater than could be accounted for by the difference in caloric intake and expenditure. O'Hara and colleagues suggested that the discrepancy in calories might be due to increases in protein synthesis and/or ketosis. An increase in the metabolic rate due to shivering might also explain why fat is used at a faster rate in the cold than in a neutral environment. Unfortunately, there is little evidence that obese women lose extra calories through shivering during or after exercise in cold water (Sheldahl, Buskirk, Loomis, & Mendez, 1982). The women failed to lose weight or body fat during the 8-week training period.

RESPONSES TO WATER IMMERSION

Water is a much better heat conductor than air. Heat is lost rapidly from the skin during water immersion. The convective heat transfer coefficient during rest in still water is 230 watts•m^{-2}•°C^{-1} (Nadel et al., 1974) and in still air is approximately 9 watts•m^{-2}•°C^{-1} (Colin, Timbal, Guieu, Boutelier, & Houdas, 1970). One method used to study the human's physiological responses to cold is determining the critical temperature, which is defined as the lowest air or water temperature that produces no increase in the resting metabolic rate over a 3-hour period. Peripheral vasoconstriction and, therefore, tissue insulation are assumed to be maximal before shivering thermogenesis is stimulated (Smith & Hanna, 1975). The critical water temperature is several degrees higher (28° to 33° C) than the critical air temperature (21° to 27° C), reflecting the greater thermal conductivity of water.

Swimming Responses

Because thermal conductivity is greater in water, the physiological responses to exercise in equivalent air and water temperatures are not always the same. In water at temperatures of 25° C and below, $\dot{V}O_2$ increases above that in 25° C air, and heart rate decreases (Craig & Dvorak, 1969; McArdle, Magel, Lesmes, & Pechar, 1976). $\dot{V}O_2$ increases because of shivering thermogenesis and possibly a decrease in mechanical efficiency during exercise. Because cardiac output increases linearly with an increase in $\dot{V}O_2$, the decrease in heart rate during exercise in cold water is more than compensated for by an increase in stroke volume (McArdle et al., 1976). Stroke volume increase is due to increased peripheral vasoconstriction in cold water. When water temperature is 30° C and above, metabolic rate and heart rate are the same in air and water environments. If the increase in stroke volume is due to the hydrostatic pressure effect of water instead of increased peripheral vasoconstriction, heart rate should be depressed in warm water.

Because heat is lost rapidly in cold water, swimming at submaximal speeds reduces core temperatures even though the metabolic rate is elevated (Holmer & Bergh, 1974; Nadel et al., 1974). The increase in metabolic rate is inversely related to water temperature. Blood lactate levels were elevated during submaximal swims in cold water, while muscle temperatures were reduced (Holmer & Bergh, 1974). Holmer and Bergh suggest that low muscle temperatures may alter the physical and chemical processes in the muscle during exercise, which decreases mechanical efficiency during swimming in cold water.

Survival in Cold Water

Exposure to extremely cold water (less than 20° C) results in a rapid increase in the metabolic rate from the stimulation of cold receptors in the skin (Hayward, Eckerson, & Collis, 1975). Such exposure may occur in a boating accident or by falling through the ice. The increase in metabolic rate accounted for one third of the heat lost while floating with a life jacket. Although swimming increases the metabolic rate 2.5 times that produced by shivering, the rate of heat loss also increases. Hayward and colleagues suggest that at water temperatures of 20° C and below a person is more likely to survive by staying still in the water rather than swimming unless the shore is very near. Heat loss from the skin is enhanced by moving water currents. Because skin temperature increases over the active muscles in the arms and legs, the thermal gradient between the skin and water increases (Hayward, Collis, & Eckerson, 1973). This augments body heat loss. The highest skin temperatures at rest in cold water are over the upper chest, lateral thorax, and groin. This is most likely because of the small amount of subcutaneous fat and muscle covering these areas and the nearness of blood vessels to the surface.

FACTORS AFFECTING RESPONSES TO COLD

There are several factors that influence a person's rate of heat loss in a cold environment, including the amount of subcutaneous fat, gender, fitness level, clothing, and wind velocity.

Skinfold Thickness

The thickness of the subcutaneous fat layer influences tissue insulation in the cold. When the cutaneous blood vessels are constricted, both the skin and underlying subcutaneous fat serve as insulation. Fat is an excellent insulator, having a thermal resistance of $0.048°$ C• m^2•$watt^{-1}$•cm^{-1} (Veicsteinas, Ferretti, & Rennie, 1982). The thermal resistance of bloodless skin is approximately 50% that of fat. The thicker the fat layer, the greater the insulation (see Figure 3.6). Skinfold thickness measures a double fold of skin and subcutaneous fat. For example if the skinfold thickness is 14 mm, 4 mm will be a double layer of skin and 10 mm will be a double layer of fat. The actual fat thickness will be 5 mm.

Tissue insulation at rest in cold air and cold water is directly proportional to the subcutaneous fat thickness (Buskirk, Thompson, & Whedon, 1963; Carlson, Hsieh, Fullington, & Elsner, 1958; Kollias et al., 1974). During exercise in a cold environment, tissue insulation is also directly related to skinfold thickness (Haymes, Dickinson, Malville, & Ross, 1982; Veicsteinas et al., 1982). Because increased tissue insulation reduces heat loss, core temperature decreases more rapidly during swimming in persons with small subcutaneous fat layers than in fatter individuals (Nadel et al., 1974; Pugh & Edholm, 1955; Sloan & Keatinge, 1975).

Because persons with more fat are better insulated against the cold, they can tolerate a lower water or air temperature before shivering than lean persons (Smith & Hanna, 1975). Metabolic rate is inversely related to body fat during cold exposure (Buskirk et al., 1963; Kollias et al., 1974). When peripheral vasoconstriction is maximal, blood flow is not only diverted from the skin but also from the superficial muscle tissues. Veicsteinas and colleagues (1982) found that the subcutaneous fat layer accounted for only a small amount of the tissue insulation at rest or during submaximal exercise in cold water. Constriction of blood vessels to the superficial muscles increases the thickness of the insulating shell. In order to achieve the same insulative thickness as

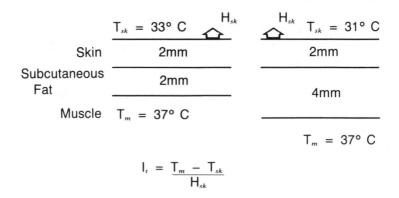

Figure 3.6. Tissue insulation.

a person with more body fat, a lean person would have to constrict blood vessels to a larger proportion of the muscle mass.

Gender

Are women better protected against the cold than men? Several studies have reported that women have lower skin temperatures than men when resting in the cold (Buskirk et al., 1963; Wyndham et al., 1964). It has been suggested that the low skin temperatures are due to women's large skinfold thicknesses. Because there is a thicker insulative shell between the blood vessels and skin, skin temperatures decrease more in women than men. Core temperature is maintained at approximately the same level in men and women resting in the cold.

It is more difficult to answer whether women are better protected against the cold during exercise than men. One of the problems in making comparisons between men and women during exercise is matching the exercise intensities. If men have higher maximal oxygen uptakes ($\dot{V}O_2$max) and both sexes exercise at the same relative intensity, the men will be exercising at a greater absolute intensity than the women. When the absolute exercise intensity is lower for women, less heat is produced through metabolism, and mean body temperature will not increase as much (Graham, 1983). If men and women exercise at the same absolute exercise intensity but the women have a smaller $\dot{V}O_2$max, relative exercise intensity is greater for the women. In this case, core temperature will be higher for the women because core temperature is directly related to relative exercise intensity.

Women also gain heat faster when exercising at the same absolute intensity as men because of their smaller body mass. As every good cook knows, the more water you put in a teakettle, the longer it takes to boil. The rate at which the water gains heat is inversely proportional to its mass or volume. Unless the heat is also lost at a faster rate from the skin, core temperature of a small person will increase more than for a large person. If women have lower skin temperatures because of increased subcutaneous fat thickness, the thermal gradient between the skin and air will be less and the rate of heat loss from the skin will be reduced. When men and women matched for skinfold thickness and $\dot{V}O_2$max are compared during exercise at the same absolute intensity, there are no differences in core and skin temperatures between the sexes (Haymes, Cartee, Rape, Garcia, & Temples, 1982).

Surface area to mass ratio affects the rate at which heat is lost from the skin. A person with a large surface area to mass ratio loses heat more rapidly than a person with a small ratio, because the heat will be closer to the surface (see Figure 3.7). Women generally have larger surface area to mass ratios than men. When men and women with similar skinfold thicknesses are compared,

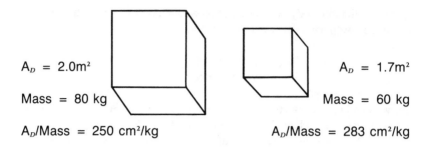

$A_D = 2.0\text{m}^2$

Mass $= 80$ kg

$A_D/\text{Mass} = 250 \text{ cm}^2/\text{kg}$

$A_D = 1.7\text{m}^2$

Mass $= 60$ kg

$A_D/\text{Mass} = 283 \text{ cm}^2/\text{kg}$

Figure 3.7. Surface area/mass ratio.

women lose heat more rapidly than men during immersion in cold water (Kollias et al., 1974). To combat the rapid heat loss, women must increase their metabolic rates to a greater extent than men.

Physical Fitness

Although it is well established that physical conditioning improves tolerance to hot environments, the relationship between fitness and tolerance to a cold environment is much less clear. Some evidence exists that training may partially acclimatize a person to the cold. Core temperature decreases to a lower level in trained distance runners than sedentary controls before shivering begins during cold exposure (Baum, Bruck, & Schwennicke, 1976). Skin temperatures in the cold have been found to both decrease (Kollias, Boileau, & Buskirk, 1972) and increase (Adams & Heberling, 1958; Keatinge, 1961) after physical training. If blood flow to the skin and T_{sk} increased in the cold, heat would be lost at a faster rate and the metabolic rate would need to increase to prevent the core temperature from decreasing. Decreased skin temperatures due to peripheral vasoconstriction, on the other hand, would increase the thermal gradient between the muscle surface and skin. By constricting skin blood vessels, more blood would be shunted to the muscles after training (Kollias et al., 1972). More studies are needed to clarify the role fitness plays in a cold environment.

Training in water (e.g., swimming) may improve cold tolerance to a greater extent than training in air (e.g., running). During exercise in 20° C water, swimmers were better able to maintain their body temperatures than runners, even though the runners increased their metabolic rates significantly more than the swimmers (McMurray & Horvath, 1979). Other factors such as differences in subcutaneous fat thickness and acclimatization may also have contributed to the swimmers' improved tolerance of cold water.

Clothing

The effective insulation afforded by clothing is a function of the air layer next to the skin, the thickness of the clothing, and the air trapped between the layers of clothing. The boundary layer of air on the surface of the clothing also provides insulation (I_a). As the environmental temperature decreases, the amount of clothing insulation needed to maintain body temperature increases (see Figure 3.8). More clothing insulation is needed during rest than during exercise at a given ambient temperature. Less insulation is needed during moderate and heavy exercise than during light exercise.

The amount of insulation provided by clothing (I_{cl}) is usually expressed in clo units. One clo has been defined as the amount of insulation needed to comfortably maintain a resting subject in a room at 20° C, humidity of less than

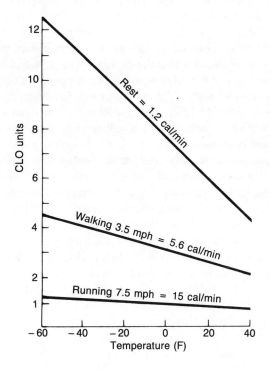

Figure 3.8 Clothing requirements at different energy expenditures in the cold.

Note. From *Physiology of Fitness*, (2nd ed.) (p. 194) by Brian Sharkey, 1984, Champaign: Human Kinetics Publishers.

50%, and air movement of 20 fpm. Clothing insulation can be calculated as follows:

$$I_{cl} = \frac{(T_{sk} - T_a)}{0.18 (E_{sw} + R + C)} - I_a.$$

During exercise, both clothing (I_{cl}) and air (I_a) insulation decrease (Belding, Russell, Darling, & Folk, 1947; Pugh, 1966b). Because the boundary layer of air moves during exercise, I_a decreases. Air insulation decreases as the velocity of air movement increases. At a velocity of 10 fpm, $I_a = 1.0$ clo, while at a velocity of 210 fpm, $I_a = 0.4$ clo (Burton & Edholm, 1955). It has been suggested that the reduction in I_{cl} during exercise is due to air movement within the clothing layers when the outer garment is wind resistant (Belding et al., 1947).

Clothing insulation is also reduced if clothing becomes wet (Pugh, 1966b). Reductions in I_{cl} up to 30% have been found as the water content of clothing increases (Hall & Polte, 1956). Because sweating may occur during exercise in a cold environment, part of the loss in clothing insulation may be due to the accumulation of sweat within the clothing. This is a problem for many athletes who exercise in the cold. Especially during periods of inactivity, heat is lost rapidly from the body if the clothing is wet. Clothing may also become wet and provide little insulation during exercise if it is raining or snowing. Outer garments that are water repellent will keep the inner layers of clothing dry and prevent heat loss.

Have you ever wondered why your feet are cold even though you are wearing boots? The insulative value of clothing covering the hands and feet is reduced when the material is compressed. Kaufman (1983) reported that compression within a boot while standing on a stone surface increases the heat loss from the foot to nearly equal that of the naked foot. Similar heat loss from the hand may occur through a glove or mitten when grasping a ski pole or ice ax. Immersion in water increases the loss in clothing insulation up to 50% because of compression (Hall & Polte, 1956).

Multiple layers of clothing are advisable during exercise in cold weather. The outer layer should be water repellent and wind resistant. Inner layers should provide insulation. Goose down is a popular insulative filler used in many outer garments worn during cold weather. Recently, several synthetic fibers have been used instead of down. There appears to be little difference in insulation among down, wool, polyester, and polyolefin (Kaufman, Bothe, & Meyer, 1982). It is not the thermal conductivity of the individual fibers but the amount of air that is trapped within the garment that provides the insulation. The innermost clothing layer should not only provide insulation but also wick moisture away from the skin to reduce evaporative heat loss. Two types of thermal underwear, polypropylene and cotton fishnet, have high wicking ability and provide excellent insulation next to the skin.

If cold exposure will be prolonged, the most clothing insulation should cover the trunk, and less insulation should cover the extremities (Kaufman, 1982). For example, a vest provides the most insulation over the trunk and less over the arms and legs during hiking or cross-country skiing. A cap or hat greatly reduces heat loss from the head.

Wind

Wind can sometimes be devastating to human survival. Convective heat loss increases as the velocity of air movement increases. Heat loss increases sharply between still air and a wind speed of 2.5 mph, and there is a more gradual increase in heat loss at higher air velocities. Total insulation decreases because of the decline in I_a. Clothing insulation particularly declines if wind penetrates the outer garments (Horvath, 1948; Pugh, 1966b). Skin temperatures decrease with wind, and the risk of frostbite increases considerably. The wind chill index is useful for evaluating the combined effects of temperature and air velocity on subjective comfort in an environment (see Table 3.3).

Table 3.3
Wind Chill Index (° C)

Wind Speed (mph)	Ambient Temperature (° C)									
	10	4	− 1	− 7	− 12	− 18	− 23	− 29	− 34	− 40
0	10	4	− 1	− 7	− 12	− 18	− 23	− 29	− 34	− 40
5	9	3	− 3	− 9	− 14	− 20	− 26	− 32	− 38	− 44
10	4	− 2	− 9	− 13	− 23	− 29	− 36	− 43	− 50	− 57
15	2	− 6	− 13	− 20	− 28	− 38	− 43	− 50	− 58	− 65
20	0	− 8	− 16	− 23	− 32	− 39	− 47	− 55	− 63	− 71
25	− 1	− 9	− 18	− 26	− 34	− 42	− 50	− 59	− 67	− 76
30	− 2	− 10	− 19	− 28	− 36	− 44	− 53	− 62	− 70	− 78
35	− 3	− 12	− 20	− 29	− 37	− 45	− 55	− 63	− 72	− 80

Little danger of freezing exposed tissues	Increasing danger of freezing exposed tissues	Great danger of freezing exposed tissues

Adapted from Sharkey, B.J., 1975, *Physiology and Physical Activity*, New York, Harper & Row Publishers, pp. 108-109. Reprinted with permission.

During rest or light exercise in a cold environment with a wind of 5 to 10 mph, shivering increases the metabolic rate to offset the increased heat loss (Horvath, 1978; Pugh, 1966b). If one's clothing is wet, convective heat loss will be so great that the body cannot produce enough extra heat through shivering to offset heat loss. Stored body heat is lost and core temperature falls (Pugh, 1967b).

A similar situation occurs during prolonged moderate exercise (55 to 60% $\dot{V}O_2$max) in a cold, windy environment if clothing insulation is not adequate. For example, when $T_a = -20°$ C and wind speed is 9.5 mph (wind chill index $= -30°$ C), an athlete who has a I_{cl} of 1.6 clo will lose heat faster than he will produce it unless energy expenditure exceeds 10 METS (Haymes, et al., 1982). In many sports (e.g., running, skiing, skating) the body moving through the air produces this same wind effect. Skin and core temperatures decrease while skiing downhill because of increased air movement past the body. Unless the outer garment is wind resistant, air will penetrate the clothing and decrease I_{cl}. Skin temperatures are better maintained in a wind and in sports where the athlete is moving if the outer garment is wind resistant (Haymes et al., 1982; Haymes & Dickinson, 1978).

ACCLIMATIZATION TO COLD

Acclimatization to cold environments has not been investigated as well as acclimatization to heat primarily because the population of cold-acclimated persons is limited. Many of the groups who live in cold climates, including the Eskimos and Lapps, have developed specialized clothing and shelters that keep them well insulated against the cold.

One of the few primitive groups that has been studied is the Australian aborigines. These people slept naked huddled between camp fires until recently, when they added clothing. Scholander and colleagues (1958) have observed two types of acclimatization to cold. One type was described as insulative because peripheral vasoconstriction increased. (The aborigines allow their skin temperatures to drop during the night and do not increase their metabolic rate, whereas Caucasians exposed to the same cold stress responded with an increase in shivering thermogenesis.) The second type of acclimatization has been described as metabolic, because the metabolic rate increases. This type of cold acclimatization occurs in Europeans after 6 weeks of cold exposure. They experienced a 50% increase in their metabolic rates during sleep and maintained their skin temperatures (Scholander, Hammel, Andersen, & Loyning, 1958).

Numerous studies have been conducted on the Korean women divers known as the ama who are exposed to 10° C water throughout the winter. These women dive for seafood all year long. Before 1977 the ama wore cotton bathing suits but have recently switched to neoprene wet suits. Compared with non-diving Korean women with similar subcutaneous fat thicknesses, the ama had a greater maximal tissue insulation and did not begin to shiver until they reached lower water and skin temperatures (Hong, 1973; Hong, Lee, Kim, Song, & Rennie, 1969). The responses suggest an insulative type of acclimatization. However, the ama also increased their basal metabolic rates (BMR) during the winter. The 30% increase in BMR could be due to an increased utilization of thyroid hormones (Hong, 1973) and to a slight increase in sensitivity to norepinephrine (Kang et al., 1970). Thyroid hormones and norepinephrine both stimulate metabolism. Kang and associates calculated a 7% increase in metabolism due to the infusion of norepinephrine.

The adoption of wet suits by the ama in 1977 led to a progressive deacclimatization to cold over the next 5 years. In 1982 the women divers' responses to cold were the same as those of Korean women nondivers. The amas' basal metabolism and maximal tissue insulation were reduced, and they shivered at the same skin temperature as the nondivers (Park et al., 1983).

Metabolic Acclimatization

Increases in metabolism during cold acclimatization may be due to nonshivering thermogenesis. Nonshivering thermogenesis is stimulated by norepinephrine in rodents. Several studies suggest that norepinephrine may play a similar role in humans after cold acclimatization. Humans have an increased sensitivity to norepinephrine after acclimatization to cold (Joy, 1963; Kang et al., 1970). After 10 months in Antarctica a decrease in norepinephrine excretion has been observed, which also suggests increased sensitivity to the hormone (Bodey, 1978). There is also some indirect evidence that nonshivering thermogenesis occurs after cold acclimatization. Davies (1961) found a decrease in shivering but no change in the metabolic rate during cold exposure after subjects had been acclimatized to the cold for 1 month.

Insulative Acclimatization

Other studies have presented evidence for an insulative type of acclimatization to cold. Scuba divers exposed to cold water maintain their core temperatures without increasing their metabolic rates, and they do not begin to shiver until they reach lower water and skin temperatures than control subjects (Skreslet & Arefjord, 1968; Hanna & Hong, 1972). Both responses suggest an increase in tissue insulation. Lower skin temperatures and decreased metabolic rates were found in a group of men who stayed in Antarctica for 1 year (Wyndham, Plotkin, & Munro 1964). Because the men gained weight during the year, the increased insulation may have been due to an increase in subcutaneous fat thickness. Increases in skinfold thickness over the trunk have been found after 10 months in Antarctica (Bodey, 1978).

It has been assumed that the increase in tissue insulation is due to increased peripheral vasoconstriction. However, Hong and associates (1969) also presented evidence for an increase in blood flow to the limbs of the ama with no increase in heat loss. They suggested that the efficiency of the countercurrent heat exchange mechanism might be increased with acclimatization.

Seasonal Acclimatization

During the winter months if a person is exposed to the cold on a regular basis, some acclimatization occurs. The T_{sk} at onset of shivering and the amount of shivering were both decreased during the winter compared with summer exposures to cold (Davies & Johnston, 1961). Athletes who spend several hours exercising in the cold each day (e.g., skiers, skaters) are more likely to be cold acclimatized than people who spend the entire day in heated buildings and drive to work in a heated car.

COLD INJURIES

Hypothermia

The most serious form of cold injury is hypothermia. As body temperature decreases, shivering is stimulated to balance heat loss with increased heat production. However, if the core temperature falls below 34° C, shivering will cease (Pugh, 1966a). Death occurs when the core temperature reaches the 23° to 25° C range (Keatinge, 1969). Accidental hypothermia is most likely to occur when a person is immersed in cold water or the clothing becomes wet in a rain or snowstorm. Hypothermia cases on land are frequently coupled with a high wind that accelerates heat loss. Pugh (1966a) found from a survey of 23 incidents of accidental hypothermia that physical exhaustion frequently preceded the most serious cases. Usually one member of the group was unable to keep up with the pace and had to be helped by others in the group. He recommended that hiking partners be matched in aerobic capacity during long hikes and sojourns in the mountains to avoid having one person set a pace that is too fast for the other members of the group. Other factors that favored the development of hypothermia included inadequate clothing for the conditions and a low percent body fat. Women were better able to survive in extreme cold weather conditions than men, probably because of women's greater percent body fat (Pugh, 1966a).

In some cases of hypothermia, hypoglycemia may precede the onset of hypothermia. Alcohol ingestion before or after exercise lowers blood glucose levels in the cold (Graham, 1981; Haight & Keatinge, 1973). Haight and

Keatinge (1973) observed that shivering did not occur in the cold after hypoglycemia developed. Both rectal and esophageal temperatures fell below 35° C as a consequence. Heat loss increases during exercise in cold air environments after alcohol is consumed (Graham, 1981). Skiers and other back-country travelers should be aware of the increased risk of hypothermia when alcohol is consumed.

Early symptoms of hypothermia are weakness, fatigue, stumbling and falling, and an inability to keep up the pace (Pugh, 1966a). Adolph and Molnar (1946) observed that once fatigue develops, shivering and metabolic heat production decrease. Later symptoms include collapse, stupor, and unconsciousness. Pugh (1964) reported that collapse usually occurs within 2 hours of the time the victim becomes unable to keep the pace. Mental symptoms are not an early indicator of hypothermia. Victims reported feeling anxious about the situation and later apathy (Pugh, 1966a). Their companions reported that the victims were irritable, aggressive, and irrational or quiet and apathetic.

Frostbite

Another type of cold injury is frostbite, the freezing of superficial tissues. Exposed areas of the body such as the face, ears, fingers, and toes are the most susceptible to frostbite, Cold-induced vasodilation frequently precedes the actual freezing of the tissue. Vasodilation increases the blood flow to the region, which elevates the temperature but also increases heat loss from the region. If the combination of wind velocity and air temperature (wind chill) is sufficient, the tissues will freeze. There is increasing danger of frostbite when the wind chill index reaches approximately −32° C.

Many persons are unaware of frostbite because the sensory nerves are blocked and the skin is numb. They may not be aware of frostbite on the fingers and toes until they remove the gloves and boots. Companions should frequently check exposed areas of the face for frostbite when the wind chill index is in the dangerous zone. Frostbite can best be treated by rewarming the part in warm water (40° C) and protecting the area from further damage and infection (Keatinge, 1969). Preventive measures include gloves and boots that provide adequate insulation for the hands and feet, hats that cover the ears, and masks or bandanas that protect the face.

EFFECTS OF COLD ON PERFORMANCE

Many sports, including skiing, ice skating, and ice hockey, are performed outdoors during cold weather. Other sports such as football, soccer, and baseball are sometimes played when the weather is cold. Mountaineers, scuba divers, and swimmers are frequently exposed to a cold environment. Performance in these sports may be altered if body temperatures decrease.

Cardiovascular Endurance

Performance in endurance activities is likely to be affected if the whole body cools. The longer a person exercises in cold air or water, the greater the risk that core and muscle temperatures will decrease. When core temperature is lowered, maximal oxygen intake is reduced (Bergh & Ekblom, 1979b; Davies, Ekblom, Bergh, & Kanstrup-Jensen, 1975; Holmer & Bergh, 1974; Nadel et al., 1974). During exercise that requires maximal aerobic power, performance times are reduced in direct proportion to the reduction in core and muscle temperatures (Bergh & Ekblom, 1979b). The reduction in $\dot{V}O_2$max is most likely due to the reduction in maximal heart rate that occurs with cooling. Even though peripheral vasoconstriction increases venous return, it is unlikely that the maximal stroke volume will increase. Decreased maximal heart rate, therefore, reduces maximal cardiac output (Rennie, Park, Veicsteinas, & Pendergast, 1980). When blood temperature decreases, the oxygen dissociation curve shifts to the left. This means that less oxygen will be unloaded at the tissues when the blood is cooled than at normal body temperature ($37°$ C). Because $\dot{V}O_2$max is the product of maximal cardiac output times the amount of O_2 unloaded at the tissues, a reduction in both factors in the cold will reduce $\dot{V}O_2$max.

Prolonged submaximal exercise bouts may also be affected by reduced core and muscle temperatures. The metabolic rate is elevated during exercise when core temperature is below normal (Nadel, Holmer, Bergh, Åstrand, & Stolwijk, 1973). For a given exercise intensity, a person would be working at a higher percentage $\dot{V}O_2$max when core temperature is reduced. Because more energy would be needed during exercise, the glycogen stores would probably be used at a faster rate than when core temperature is normal. This could lead to an earlier onset of fatigue. Blood to the muscle is reduced during exercise when the body is cooled (Rennie et al., 1980). Because a reduction in blood flow reduces the delivery of oxygen to the muscles, more anaerobic energy is needed in the cold, and lactate formation would increase.

Strength and Power

Activities that require strength and power are affected by peripheral cooling of muscles and nerves. Cooling of muscles reduces the peak torque (force produced during dynamic exercise, especially at faster velocities (Bergh & Ekblom,

1979a). The amount of power produced is a function of both torque and angular velocity,

$$P = T \times w,$$
  where P = power
        T = torque
        w = angular velocity

Performances in jumping and sprinting events, both power events, are reduced by decreases in muscle temperature (Asmussen, Bonde-Petersen, & Jorgensen, 1976; Bergh & Ekblom, 1979a).

There are several possible reasons why cooling may inhibit force production. The reduction in torque may be due to an increase in the time it takes for the muscle fibers to reach maximal tension with cooling (Davies, Mecrow, & White, 1982). It has been suggested that the rate at which the crossbridges from the myosin to the actin break and reattach may be slowed as the muscle cools (Asmussen et al., 1976). Another possible explanation is an increase in fluid viscosity. As the temperature of the muscle decreases, the viscosity of the sarcoplasm (fluid inside the muscle fiber) increases, which increases the resistance to movement of the crossbridges and actin. Chemical reactions also slow down as the temperature decreases. ATP utilization decreases at low muscle temperatures (Edwards et al., 1972).

Although dynamic strength decreases with muscle cooling, the effect on isometric strength is less clear. Several studies have reported no significant decline in isometric strength with muscle cooling (Asmussen et al., 1976; Bergh & Ekblom, 1979a; Binkhorst, Hoofd, & Vissers, 1977), while others have reported loss of muscle strength when the muscle temperature was below 30° C (Clarke, Hellon, & Lind, 1958; Davies et al., 1982). At low skin temperatures nerve conduction velocity decreases (Marshall, 1972; Vanggaard, 1975). When the skin temperature falls below 6° C, supramaximal stimulation of the motor nerves produces no muscle action potentials, which suggests that nerve conduction has been blocked. The studies that demonstrated decreased isometric strength with cooling used water baths that lowered skin temperatures to less than 6° C. If nerve conduction to the superficial muscle fibers is blocked, fewer muscle fibers would contract, and isometric strength would decrease.

Muscular Endurance

Muscular endurance is enhanced by slight cooling but reduced by severe cold. Fatigue develops within the muscle at a slower rate with cooling (Bundschuh & Clarke, 1982; Davies et al., 1982). On the other hand, heating the muscle decreases muscular endurance (Edwards et al., 1972). As skin temperature increases, blood flow is diverted to the skin, which reduces muscle blood flow and slows the removal of metabolic waste products. When muscle temperature falls below 27° C, muscular endurance decreases. The decline in muscle endurance at T_m below 27° C is thought to be due to reduced nerve conduction and the recruitment of fewer muscle fibers, especially those nearest the muscle surface (Clarke et al., 1958).

SUMMARY

Humans use two physiological defense mechanisms in cold environments: increased metabolism (shivering thermogenesis) and increased tissue insulation (vasoconstriction). Both appear to be stimulated by cooling skin thermoreceptors. During exercise in the cold, heat loss is facilitated by the increased temperature gradient between the skin and environment. Unless the body is adequately insulated by subcutaneous fat or by clothing, heat loss may exceed heat gain and whole body cooling will occur.

Water is an excellent conductor of heat, and heat loss accelerates during immersion and when clothing is wet. Wind or movement of the body through air or water (e.g., running or swimming) also increases the rate of heat loss. Survival in extremely cold water is prolonged when a person remains motionless. To protect against the wind and moisture, the outer layer of clothing should be both wind and water resistant. Inner layers of clothing should provide adequate insulation for the level of physical activity. More insulation is needed during light activity than during heavy exercise.

Excessive body heat loss reduces the core temperature and may lead to hypothermia. Hypothermia is frequently preceded by physical exhaustion and, in some cases, hypoglycemia. Fatigue, weakness, stumbling, and falling are early symptoms of hypothermia. Exposed skin areas are susceptible to frostbite, especially when the wind chill index reaches −32° and below. Because the skin is numb, many victims are unaware of frostbite on the face, toes, and fingers. Frostbite can best be prevented by wearing gloves and boots with adequate insulation, hats that cover the ears, and masks or bandanas that cover the face.

Maximal aerobic capacity and endurance are reduced when the core temperature falls below normal. Performance in events that require dynamic muscle strength and power decreases as muscle temperatures decrease. It is, therefore, advantageous to keep the body warm before and during activities that require muscle strength and power or cardiovascular endurance. Muscular endurance may be enhanced by slight muscle cooling, but it is hampered by drastic cooling. Clothing with enough insulation to prevent the core from cooling should be worn during endurance activities.

4

Altitude and Performance

This chapter examines the effects of reduced atmospheric pressure on physiological responses during rest and exercise. We will examine how the physical environment is changed at altitude and discuss the effects of chronic exposure to hypoxia.

Many sea level residents participate in skiing, hiking, and mountain climbing at moderate altitudes, and some of them will suffer from altitude illnesses shortly after they arrive. We will discuss how to recognize and prevent the symptoms. In some sporting events performance actually improves at altitude. For example, sprinters run faster at altitude than at sea level. Unfortunately, in other events performance is likely to be hindered by reduced atmospheric pressures.

The following questions will be discussed in this chapter:

- Why does it seem that exercise is more tiring at altitude than at sea level?
- How is the physical environment changed at altitude?
- How does the body respond to reduced oxygen pressure (hypoxia)?
- Why is maximal exercise reduced at altitude?
- Will a person adapt to altitude after a period of time?
- Will training at altitude be beneficial to performance on returning to sea level?

PHYSICS OF ALTITUDE

Is there less oxygen in the air at altitude than at sea level? The barometric pressure (P_B) at altitude is less than at sea level (760 mm Hg or torr; 1 torr = 1 mm Hg). Air pressure decreases as the weight of the column of air above the point of measurement decreases. The decrease in barometric pressure is exponential with increase in altitude. At an altitude of 5,500 meters (18,000 feet) above sea level the barometric pressure decreases by 50% to 390 torr (see Figure 4.1). The percentage of oxygen remains relatively constant at

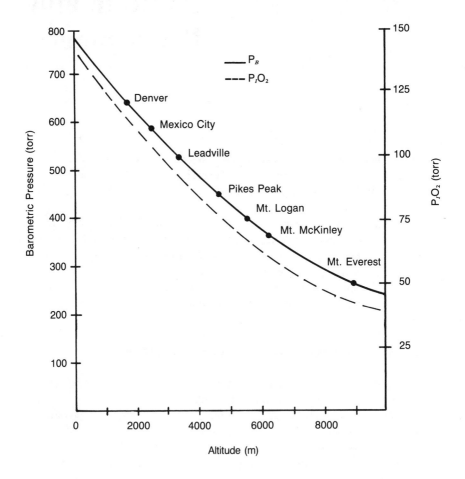

Figure 4.1 Barometric pressure (P_B) and inspired PO_2 (P_IO_2) at different altitudes.

Note. From Exercise and altitude (p. 212) by J. Kollias and E.R. Buskirk, 1974. In W.R. Johnson and E.R. Buskirk (Eds.) *Science and medicine in exercise and sport* (2nd ed.). New York: Harper & Row. Adapted with permission.

20.93% as altitude increases. However, because P_B decreases, the pressure of oxygen in the inspired air (P_{IO_2}) decreases (see Figure 4.1). This is because

$P_{IO_2} = (P_B - 47 \text{ torr}) \times .2093,$

where 47 torr represents the pressure of water vapor in the lungs at body temperature.

Oxygen pressure in the inspired air decreases by 50% to 75 torr at an altitude of 5,000 meters (16,400 feet). Oxygen pressure has been estimated to be approximately 39 torr at the summit of Mt. Everest (8,848 meters).

Why does the air feel colder at the top than at the base of a mountain? Air temperature decreases at the rate of 6° C per 1,000 meters (m) increase in altitude. Solar radiation, however, increases with altitude, because air pollution and cloud cover diminish and more ultraviolet radiation is able to penetrate the atmosphere. The presence of snow at high altitudes also increases solar radiation, because ultraviolet rays are reflected by snow. This is especially true of the ultraviolet rays UV-B (wave length of 290 to 320 nm), which produce corneal inflammation and sunburn. At an altitude of 3,000 m, UV-B is twice that at 700 m and may double again if the ground is covered by snow (Buettner & Slonin, 1974).

Will a golf ball travel farther at altitude than at sea level? Gravity decreases as the square of the distance from the center of the earth. At sea level, acceleration due to gravity (g) is 9.8 m•sec^{-2}. The decrease in acceleration due to gravity with increased altitude is 0.003086 m•sec^{-2} per 1,000 m increase in elevation. Acceleration due to gravity is also affected by latitude, which is lowest at the equator and highest at the north and south poles. In Mexico City (altitude = 2,300 m), acceleration due to gravity is 9.779 m•sec^{-2}. Because gravitational force determines the time it takes a freely falling body to strike earth, the time of flight and distance covered by a projectile will increase as altitude increases. The time of flight (t) is determined by the velocity in a vertical direction (V_y) and g,

$t = 2V_y•g^{-1}.$

The horizontal distance covered by a projectile (d) is determined by the velocity of the projectile in both the vertical and horizontal (V_x) directions and g,

$d = V_x \times 2V_y•g^{-1},$ or
$d = V_x \times t.$

Balls travel farther as altitude increases because they remain in flight for a longer time.

Movement of a projectile or body through the air is also affected by the amount of air resistance encountered. Air resistance results in two types of air flow around an object: laminar flow and turbulent flow. Laminar flow results in smooth layers of air moving by the object, while turbulent flow produces eddies behind the object. Resistance to flow (R) is directly proportional to air velocity for laminar flow but increases as the square of the air velocity for turbulent flow:

$$R = k_1v + k_2v^2,$$
   where k_1 and k_2 are constants and v is the air velocity.

Air flow changes from laminar to turbulent when Reynold's number exceeds 2,000. Reynold's number is a dimensionless constant that is directly proportional to the object's diameter, air velocity, and air density and inversely related to viscosity. Because air density decreases as the barometric pressure decreases, Reynold's number is less at altitude than at sea level. This increases the air velocity needed for turbulent air flow. Resistance to air flow decreases because more of the air flow is laminar.

Reduction in air density reduces the amount of work that must be done by the respiratory muscles to overcome airway resistance during breathing as altitude increases. It will also reduce the air resistance encountered by runners, skiers, and cyclists.

ACUTE PHYSIOLOGICAL RESPONSES

The main factor affecting the human's physiological responses to altitude is the decrease in barometric pressure and the associated decline in inspired PO_2. Gas molecules move from a region of higher pressure to one of lower pressure. Because the inspired PO_2 decreases with altitude, the alveolar PO_2 (P_AO_2 also declines (see Table 4.1). This means that the oxygen pressure gradient between the alveoli and venous blood is reduced at altitude. The result is lower PO_2 in the arterial blood. Chemoreceptors known as the aortic and carotid bodies, located in the aorta and carotid arteries, are sensitive to changes in arterial PO_2 (P_aO_2), especially to decreased arterial PO_2 and they send nerve impulses to the brain to increase ventilation. By increasing ventilation, more oxygen is brought into the lungs every minute for exchange with the blood.

Most of the oxygen that diffuses through the alveoli into the blood is not dissolved in the plasma but is bound to hemoglobin in the red blood cells. The amount of oxygen that is bound to hemoglobin is determined by the shape of the oxygen dissociation curve and the arterial PO_2. At sea level the arterial PO_2 is 100 torr, and the saturation of hemoglobin with oxygen (SaO_2) is 96% (see Table 4.1 and Figure 4.2). When the arterial PO_2 decreases at altitude, hemoglobin saturation decreases little at first, because the curve is relatively flat at the higher PO_2 levels. On top of Pikes Peak (4,300 meters), arterial PO_2 is 44 torr and hemoglobin saturation with oxygen decreases to 82% (Vogel & Hansen, 1967). This reduces the amount of oxygen carried by the blood

Table 4.1

Oxygen Pressures and Saturation at Various Altitudes

Pressures	Sea Level	Leadville	Pikes Peak	Mt. Everest
Altitude (m)	0	3,100	4,300	8,848
P_B (torr)	760	530	440	250
P_IO_2 (torr)	150	101	82	42
P_AO_2 (torr)	105	71	47	30
PaO$_2$ (mm Hg)	100	52	44	25
SaO$_2$ (%)	96	90	82	48

Data compiled from Grover (1978), Hannon (1978), Vogel and Hansen (1967), and West (1982).

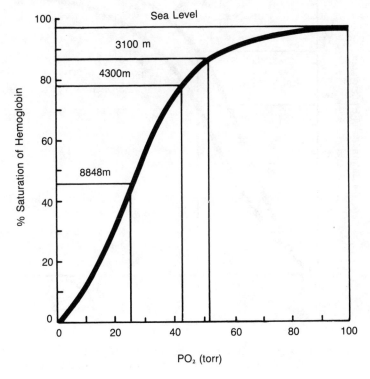

Figure 4.2 Standard oxygen dissociation curve for blood pH = 7.4 and temperature = 37° C. Vertical lines indicate PO$_2$ and horizontal lines indicate percent hemoglobin saturation of arterial blood at sea level, 3,100 m, 4,300 m, and 8,848 m.

Note. From Physiological adaptations to high altitude (p. 333) by R.F. Grover, 1979, In *Sports Medicine and Physiology*, R.H. Strauss (Ed.) Philadelphia: W.B. Saunders Co. Reprinted with permission.

by 14%. Because each gram of hemoglobin holds 1.34 ml of oxygen when fully saturated, the actual oxygen content (CaO_2) of the blood is determined by both the level of hemoglobin saturation (SaO_2) and the amount of hemoglobin (Hb) present:

$$CaO_2 = SaO_2 \times Hb \times 1.34 \text{ ml } O_2 \cdot g \ Hb^{-1}.$$

Oxygen delivery to the tissues is determined by two factors: the amount of blood flow to the tissues and the tissue oxygen pressure. Tissue oxygen pressure determines the amount of oxygen that will be unloaded by hemoglobin when the blood flows through the capillaries (see Figure 4.3). Blood flow to the tissues is determined by the cardiac output and the number of open capillaries in the tissue. At rest only about 15% to 20% of the cardiac output is directed to skeletal muscles, and most of the capillaries are closed. Cardiac

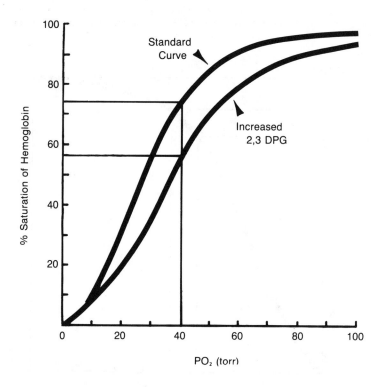

Figure 4.3 Standard oxygen dissociation curve for blood pH = 7.4 and temperature = 37° C and curve shifted to right with increased 2, 3 DPG concentration, decreasing affinity of Hb for O_2.

Note. From Physiology of Respiration (2nd ed.) (p. 185) by J.H. Comroe, 1974, Chicago: Year Book Medical Publishers. Adapted with permission.

output can increase by increasing either heart rate or stroke volume or both. When a person arrives at altitude, cardiac output at rest increases primarily because of an increase in heart rate (Vogel & Hansen, 1967). As Figure 4.2 shows, cardiac output at 4,300 m would need to increase 14% to compensate for the 14% reduction in hemoglobin saturation with oxygen. Oxygen delivery to the tissues at rest is maintained at an altitude of 4,300 m by increasing ventilation and cardiac output. At an elevation of 7,850 m, Pugh (1964a) estimated that arterial PO_2 would not exceed 30 torr, because the measured alveolar PO_2 was 32 torr. This would reduce hemoglobin saturation to 60% and necessitate a 36% increase in cardiac output at rest to maintain oxygen delivery to the tissues.

Changes in Blood Components

Hemoglobin concentration increases during the first 2 days of exposure to altitude. Initially the increase in hemoglobin is due to a decrease in plasma volume; however, the bone marrow increases iron uptake for hemoglobin formation during the first 48 hours at altitude (Reynafarje, Lozano, & Valdiviesto, 1959). The increase in hemoglobin concentration increases the amount of oxygen carried per deciliter (dl) (1 dl = 100 ml) of blood. If the hemoglobin concentration was 15 gm•dl^{-1} at sea level and increased 20% at altitude to 18 gm•dl^{-1}, the CaO_2 would also increase 20%. Hemoglobin concentration increased 20% after 1 week at an altitude of 3,940 m and was accompanied by a 14% decrease in plasma volume (Buskirk, Kollias, Picon-Reatigue, Akers, Prokop, & Baker, 1967). Because the increase in hemoglobin increases the amount of oxygen delivered to the tissues, resting cardiac output and heart rate decrease toward sea level values after a few days at altitude. While loss of plasma volume has a positive effect in increasing the CaO_2, it has a negative effect on blood flow. Decreased plasma volume increases the viscosity of the blood, especially when the hematocrit rises about 50%. Increased viscosity means increased resistance to blood flow, which will increase the amount of work done by the heart. Forced hydration prevents plasma volume from decreasing and the hemoglobin concentration remains constant during the first week of altitude exposure (Greenleaf, Bernauer, Adams, & Juhos, 1978).

Within the red blood cells, the concentration of 2,3 diphosphoglycerate (2,3 DPG) increases during the first 24 hours at altitude (Lenfant, et al., 1968). The effect of increasing the 2,3 DPG level is to shift the oxygen dissociation curve to the right (see Figure 4.3). This means that more oxygen would be unloaded at the tissues at any given capillary PO_2. Increased 2,3 DPG levels offset the tendency for the curve to shift to the left because of the lowering of the arterial PCO_2. Hyperventilation due to hypoxia will increase the amount of CO_2 blown off from the lungs, which lowers alveolar and arterial PCO_2

levels. If the oxygen dissociation curve was allowed to shift to the left, less oxygen would leave the blood and enter the tissues for a given PO_2.

Fluid Balance

Body weight usually decreases during the first 2 weeks at altitudes of 3,000 m and above (Buskirk et al., 1967; Consolazio, Johnson, & Kryzwicki, 1972). Part of the initial weight loss is due to loss of appetite and a decrease in caloric intake. Total body water is also decreased at altitude (Buskirk et al., 1967). Water loss through the kidneys increases, especially when it is cold. A small part of the water loss is due to increased respiratory evaporation.

Vapor pressure of the air decreases as altitude increases. During inspiration, the vapor pressure of the inspired air increases to 47 torr by the addition of water from the respiratory tract. During exhalation, most of this water vapor is lost. Because ventilation also increases at altitude, the amount of water vapor lost through the respiratory tract is much greater than that at sea level. Dehydration is fairly common among mountain climbers. Pugh (1964a) found that climbers lost 2.9 gm of water per 100 L of air (BTPS) at an altitude of 5,500 m. The average ventilation of climbers ascending at their normal pace at this altitude is 88 L(BTPS)•min^{-1} (Pugh, 1958). The estimated respiratory water loss during 7 hours of climbing would be 1,072 ml. Resting ventilation at 5,500 m is approximately 19 L(BTPS)•min^{-1}. After 17 hr this would contribute an additional 562 ml of water loss, for a total of 1,634 ml per day. Pugh (1964a) recommended that climbers consume 3 to 4 L of fluid per day "to maintain a urine output of 1.5 L per day."

There is evidence that men and women do not increase their water intakes enough to balance water loss at altitude. Body weight losses of 3.5 to 4.0 kg have been reported for men during a 12-day period at 4,300 m (Consolazio et al., 1972). Body water loss accounted for approximately 50% of the weight loss, and loss of body fat, protein, and minerals accounted for the remainder. During 7 days' exposure to 4,300 m, women maintained their sea level water intake of one L per day, but body weight loss averaged 1.0 kg for the week (Hannon, Klain, Sudman, & Sullivan, 1976). Although the women consumed fewer calories at 4,300 m than at sea level, the caloric deficit accounted for less than half of the weight loss, which suggests that the remaining weight loss was due to water loss and that water intake should be increased at altitude.

Acid/Base Balance

The loss of excess CO_2 through hyperventilation decreases the amount of CO_2 in the blood. Part of the lost CO_2 is bound to hemoglobin and a small amount is dissolved in the plasma, but most of it is in the form of H_2CO_3 (carbonic acid) and HCO_3^- (bicarbonate),

$$CO_2 + H_2 \rightleftharpoons H_2CO_3 \rightleftharpoons H^+ + HCO_3^-.$$

A reduction in CO_2 reduces the amount of acid (H^+) and increases the pH of the blood. The result is respiratory alkalosis. To compensate for the loss of acid, excess base in the form of bicarbonate (HCO_3^-) must be removed from the blood. Plasma bicarbonate levels decrease during the first 2 days at altitude (Hannon, 1978). Excess bicarbonate is removed from the blood by the kidneys and excreted into the urine.

RESPONSES TO EXERCISE

Maximal Oxygen Uptake

The early onset of fatigue that occurs with exercise at altitude is not without cause. It is universally agreed that maximal oxygen uptake ($\dot{V}O_2max$) decreases at altitudes above 1,500 m. Recent evidence suggests that $\dot{V}O_2max$ declines above 1,200 m (Squires & Buskirk, 1982). Buskirk et al. (1967) reported that $\dot{V}O_2max$ decreases 3.2% per 1,000 ft above 5,000 ft. This would mean that $\dot{V}O_2max$ on Pikes Peak at an altitude of 4,300 m (14,100 ft) would be reduced approximately 29%. Actual measurements of the decrement in $\dot{V}O_2max$ at 4,300 m have yielded reductions of 27% (Young, Evans, Cymerman, Pandolf, Knapik, & Mahler, 1982) and 30% (Horstman, Weiskopf, & Jackson, 1980). Predicted and actual decreases in $\dot{V}O_2max$ reported for several altitudes are presented in Table 4.2.

The reason for the decline in maximal oxygen uptake at altitude is the reduction in oxygen content of the arterial blood (CaO_2). Initially, CaO_2 is reduced because of the reduction in barometric pressure and P_iO_2 at altitude. Both the arterial and venous PO_2 are reduced at altitude during heavy exercise, but the reduction in venous PO_2 is small compared with the decrease in arterial PO_2 (see Figure 4.4). Because hemoglobin saturation depends on the PO_2, the decline in venous oxygen content is relatively small. During maximal exercise the oxygen content of the venous blood cannot decrease enough to compensate for the lower CaO_2. The difference in arterial and venous oxygen content ($a - \bar{v}O_2$ difference) is reduced at altitude. Because $\dot{V}O_2max$ is a function of both maximal cardiac output ($\dot{Q}max$) and the $a - \bar{v}O_2$ difference,

$$\dot{V}O_2max = \dot{Q}max \times a - \bar{v}O_2 \text{ difference,}$$

a reduction in the $a - \bar{v}O_2$ difference reduces $\dot{V}O_2max$ unless $\dot{Q}max$ increases.

Table 4.2

Reduction in $\dot{V}O_2$max at Different Altitudes

Altitude	Predicted Reduction*	Actual Reduction	Study
1,219 m	0%	4.8%	Squires & Buskirk, 1982
1,524 m	0%	6.9%	Squires & Buskirk, 1982
2,300 m	8.3%	13.0%	Faulkner et al., 1968
3,100 m	16.6%	20.0%	Faulkner et al., 1968
4,300 m	29.1%	29.0%	Faulkner et al., 1968
5,800 m	44.8%	39.0%	Pugh et al., 1964
6,400 m	51.2%	45.0%	Pugh et al., 1964
7,440 m	62.0%	60.0%	Pugh et al., 1964

*Predicted decline in $\dot{V}O_2$max (%) = (Altitude [ft] − 5000)/1,000 × 3.2%.

Maximal Cardiac Output

When a person arrives at altitude, maximal cardiac output is the same as it was at sea level (Horstman et al., 1980) even though maximal heart rate has been reported to be slightly lower at altitude. This implies that maximal stroke volume is maintained or even increased initially at altitude. However, after several weeks residence at altitudes of 4,300 m and above, maximal stroke volume and cardiac output decline (Horstman et al., 1980; Pugh, 1964a). Hemoconcentration increases the arterial oxygen content during the same time period, which allows $\dot{V}O_2$max to increase slightly but does not restore $\dot{V}O_2$max to sea level values (Horstman et al., 1980). The decrease in maximal stroke volume is most likely due to the reduction in venous return, which is caused by the increased peripheral resistance from the increased blood viscosity. When red blood cells are removed from the blood, the hematocrit is reduced. Because reducing the hematocrit decreases the viscosity and resistance, maximal stroke volume and cardiac output increase (Horstman et al., 1980).

Ventilation and Diffusion Capacity

Although you may feel that breathing is more difficult at altitude, in fact you are able to move more air in and out of the lungs than at sea level. Maximal ventilation ($\dot{V}_E$ max) expressed as BTPS increases at altitude as does the max-

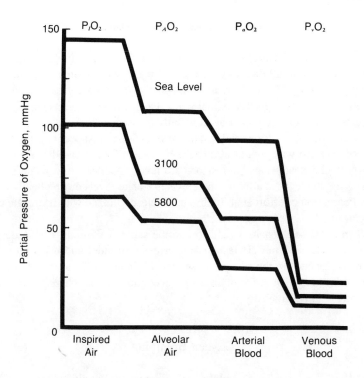

Figure 4.4. Partial pressure of oxygen in inspired air, alveolar air, arterial and venous blood during heavy exercise at different altitudes.

Note. Data compiled from "Effects of acute through life-long hypoxic exposure on exercise pulmonary gas exchange" by Dempsey et al., 1971. *Respiration Physiology,* **13**, 62-89; and "Muscular exercise at great altitudes," by Pugh et al., 1964, *Journal of Applied Physiology,* **19**, 431-440.

imal voluntary ventilation (MVV). Increased ventilation raises the alveolar PO_2 and increases the O_2 gradient between the alveoli and venous blood, thereby enhancing the transfer of O_2 to the blood. Lung diffusion capacity affects the amount of O_2 that can be transported from the lungs to the blood. During exercise lung diffusion capacity increases because more of the lung surface area is perfused with blood. However, lung diffusion capacity does not increase at altitude even after several weeks' exposure and is no greater during exercise than at sea level (DeGraff, Grover, Johnson, Hammond, & Miller, 1970). West (1982) showed that diffusion capacity limits $\dot{V}O_2$max at very high altitudes (e.g., Mt. Everest) and suggested that climbers who succeed at high altitude probably have large diffusion capacities. It has also been suggested that athletes who experience the greatest decline in $\dot{V}O_2$max at altitude have the smallest diffusion capacities (Pugh, 1967a; Saltin, 1967).

Oxygen Uptake and Lactate

Although a bout of exercise may feel more strenuous at altitude, oxygen uptake is the same at altitude as at sea level for the same submaximal absolute exercise intensity. However, heart rate and $\dot{V}_E$ (BTPS) are greater at altitude than at sea level during submaximal work. During heavy exercise muscle and blood lactate levels are higher at altitude than at sea level (Knuttgen & Saltin, 1973). Knuttgen & Saltin found that the oxygen deficit that occurs at the beginning of exercise was greater at altitude because $\dot{V}O_2$ increased more slowly and reached a steady state later than at sea level. Increased oxygen deficit increases oxygen debt at altitude and elevates lactate levels during heavy exercise. Perception of effort at altitude is more closely linked with heart rate than oxygen uptake.

When exercise intensity is adjusted to the same $\%\dot{V}O_2$max at altitude and sea level, $\dot{V}O_2$ and muscle lactate are lower at altitude, and heart rate, $\dot{V}_E$, and blood lactate are the same as at sea level (Knuttgen & Saltin, 1973). Oxygen deficit and debt are similar at sea level and altitude when exercising at the same relative intensity.

Oxygen Breathing

Until 1978 it had been assumed that Mt. Everest could only be conquered by breathing supplementary oxygen. Hillary and Tensing were the first to reach the summit in 1953. They used oxygen during the climb from 8,500 m to the summit at 8,848 m (Pugh, 1964a). In 1978 Messner and Habeler were the first climbers to reach the summit of Mt. Everest without breathing oxygen. The reason most climbers have needed oxygen above 8,500 m is the low PO_2 of the inspired air. The oxygen pressure gradient from the alveoli to the capillary blood is small even during maximal exercise. West (1982) estimated that $\dot{V}O_2$max would be below 700 ml•min^{-1} on the summit of Mt. Everest. Because resting oxygen uptake is about 250 ml•min^{-1} (1 MET), the amount of exercise would be limited to less than 3 METs. Breathing oxygen reduces both heart rate and ventilation during climbing and increases the amount of work that can be done (Pugh, 1964a).

Because breathlessness is a problem during exercise, oxygen breathing is sometimes used by athletes after exercise at much lower altitudes (e.g., 1,600 m). It is doubtful that oxygen breathing during recovery from exercise is of any benefit for removing waste products. To be of greatest value, oxygen would have to be breathed during the performance, which in most cases is not practical.

ACCLIMATIZATION TO ALTITUDE

Oxygen Transport

How long does it take a person to become fully acclimatized to an altitude? Some physiological adaptations, such as the shift in the oxygen dissociation curve that is due to increased 2,3-DPG levels in the red blood cells, begin almost immediately. Increased red blood cell production also begins immediately, but it takes approximately 2 months before blood volume increases above that at sea level. Low oxygen levels in the blood (hypoxemia) stimulate the kidneys to produce erythropoietin, which stimulates the red bone marrow to increase its production of erythrocytes (red blood cells). The bone marrow increases iron uptake to form hemoglobin after 48 hours at altitude (Reynafarje et al., 1959). However, the increase in red cell volume is accompanied by a decline in plasma volume. The net result is that blood volume does not increase during the first 2 months at altitude. Red blood cell volume continues to increase for at least 1 year and probably longer, because blood volume is greater in high-altitude natives than in sojourners even after 1 year of acclimatization (Reynafarje et al., 1959).

If red blood cell volume increases during acclimatization, then the oxygen content of the blood will also increase. Theoretically, maximal oxygen intake and the capacity for prolonged work should be greater after acclimatization. Horstman et al. (1980) found that the arterial oxygen content increased 19% after 2 weeks at 4,300 m, but maximal oxygen intake increased by only 10%. The smaller increase in $\dot{V}O_2$max after acclimatization was due to a 9% decrease in maximal stroke volume. Unfortunately, increasing the red blood cell volume (polycythemia) increases the viscosity of the blood, which increases resistance to blood flow. Venous return to the heart is reduced, which reduces stroke volume.

Respiration

Changes in respiration also occur during acclimatization to altitude. Ventilation increases shortly after arrival at altitude, which increases the alveolar PO_2. Over several weeks at altitude the alveolar to arterial oxygen gradient during exercise increases and the arterial PO_2 decreases (Dempsey et al., 1971). In contrast, high-altitude natives hypoventilate and maintain a smaller alveolar to arterial oxygen gradient. High-altitude natives are apparently better able to maintain arterial PO_2 at altitude because they have a higher diffusion capacity of the lung, a higher pulmonary capillary blood flow, and a smaller lung dead space. Sea level natives who have lived at altitude since childhood have pulmonary responses similar to those of high-altitude natives.

Hyperventilation in sea level natives after a few weeks at altitude is accompanied by a decline in arterial PCO_2. Peripheral chemoreceptors are stimulated by increased arterial PCO_2 (hypercapnia) and depressed by decreased arterial PCO_2 (hypocapnia). Decreased arterial PO_2 and pH also stimulate the peripheral chemoreceptors. Central chemoreceptors located in the brain stem are bathed by cerebral spinal fluid (CSF). Decreases in CSF pH stimulate the central chemoreceptors to increase respiration. The increase in ventilation at altitude is primarily due to the decrease in arterial PO_2; however, hypocapnia should depress the response. Because CO_2 crosses the blood-brain barrier, hypocapnia increases both arterial and CSF pH. To prevent the CSF pH from increasing (becoming alkaline), bicarbonate is excreted from the CSF. This allows hyperventilation to persist during acclimatization. The sensitivity of the peripheral chemoreceptors to PO_2 may also increase during acclimatization.

Acclimatization Limits

Is there an altitude above which humans can no longer acclimatize? The highest permanent settlement is located at 5,200 m in the Andes. Miners who live in the village climb to the mines located at 5,500 m each day, but they descend at night to sleep. Scientific expeditions have spent up to 6 months at 5,800 m, and mountain climbers have spent several weeks at 6,500 m. It has generally been observed that acclimatization stops and physical condition begins to deteriorate at altitudes above 5,200 m (17,000 ft). A progressive loss in body weight of 1 $kg \cdot wk^{-1}$ was observed in a group of men who spent 6 months at 5,800 m (Pugh, 1964a). The group's fitness for climbing was reduced at the end of the 6 month stay. Impairment of mental function has been observed at altitudes of 5,200 m and above. Visual acuity, memory, and computational and decision-making skills are all reduced from the lack of oxygen (McFarland, 1972). Sleep disturbances are also common at altitudes above 5,200 m.

There are a number of mountain peaks above 5,200 m in North America, including Mt. Logan in Canada and Mt. McKinley in Alaska. Climbers preparing to ascend the highest mountain peaks (e.g., Mt. Everest, K2) will not gain—and are likely to lose—acclimatization the more time they spend above 5,200 m. Climbing parties should plan to spend enough time at slightly lower altitudes to fully acclimatize before making the final ascent to the peak.

ALTITUDE ILLNESSES

Rapid ascent to altitudes of 2,100 m (7,000 ft) and above may precipitate one or more forms of altitude illness. Many ski areas in the western United States are located at altitudes above 2,100 m. Most of the hiking trails in Rocky Mountain and Yellowstone National Parks and on Mount Rainier are also above this altitude. Because of the popularity of skiing, hiking, and climbing, many persons coming from sea level fly to nearby airports and rapidly ascend to these moderate altitudes. This rapid gain in altitude increases the risk of altitude illness. There are several forms of altitude illness: acute mountain sickness, high-altitude pulmonary edema, high-altitude cerebral edema, and retinal hemorrhage.

Acute Mountain Sickness

Acute mountain sickness (AMS) is the most common form of altitude illness at altitudes of 2,100 m and above. Symptoms include headache, anorexia, nausea, vomiting, dizziness, insomnia, breathlessness at rest, reduced urine output, and weakness. AMS occurs 12 to 36 hours after arriving at altitude and usually lasts for 2 to 3 days. Frequency increases as the altitude increases and is more common at altitudes above 3,000 m (10,000 ft). How rapidly a person ascends to altitude influences both the incidence of AMS and the severity of the symptoms (Hackett, Rennie, & Levine, 1976). A person who drives or flys directly to moderate altitude is more likely to develop AMS than a person who hikes to that same altitude or spends several days at lower altitudes (staging) before arriving at moderate altitude. Symptom severity is directly related to the amount of altitude gained per day.

Treatment of AMS generally consists of rest, aspirin, and fluid replacement. Usually the symptoms disappear after 2 or 3 days. Measures to prevent AMS include a slow ascent to altitude during climbing (no more than 300 m per day), spending several days at lower altitudes before ascending to high altitude, use of acetazolamide (Diamox) when flying to altitudes above 2,400 m, increasing fluid intake so that the urine does not become too concentrated, and increasing the amount of carbohydrate in the diet. It has also been suggested that a person should "work high but sleep low." Many ski trails in the Rockies are located at 3,000 m and higher, but lodging is located about 2,400 m. Although skiers spend 6 or more hours on the ski slopes, they sleep at a lower altitude.

Acetazolamide is particularly effective in reducing the incidence and severity of AMS in persons who must ascend to altitude rapidly (Hackett et al., 1976). Acetazolamide elevates the blood CO_2 levels, which reduces the pH. To be effective it must be taken the day before ascent and the first day at altitude. Increasing the carbohydrate intake to 70% of the total caloric intake also reduces the severity of AMS (Consolazio, Matoush, Johnson, Krzywicki, Daws, & Isaac, 1969). Elevated carbohydrate intake increases the production of CO_2 and elevates PCO_2 levels. It also increases the amount of energy produced per liter of oxygen used.

High-Altitude Pulmonary Edema

High-altitude pulmonary edema (HAPE) is a far more serious and life-threatening problem than AMS. It usually does not occur at altitudes below 2,700 m. Symptoms include dyspnea, cough, tachycardia, headache, weakness, and frothy or bloody sputum. Children and adolescents are more likely to develop HAPE than adults. HAPE develops 1 to 3 days after arrival at altitude and can occur in altitude acclimatized persons who have descended to a lower altitude for a few days and then reascended rapidly.

Because of the seriousness of HAPE, the person should descend to a lower altitude immediately. Medical treatment is necessary because HAPE may result in death if left untreated. Preventive measures include a slow ascent during climbing with stops of several days at lower altitudes to acclimatize. A rapid ascent to altitude increases the incidence of HAPE. Strenuous exercise should be avoided during the first few days at altitudes above 2,700 m if a person has ascended rapidly to altitude (i.e., arrived by airplane).

High-Altitude Cerebral Edema

High-altitude cerebral edema (HACE) is less common than either AMS or HAPE and usually occurs at altitudes above 4,300 m. It is a serious problem and can lead to death. The symptoms include severe headache, ataxia, hallucinations, mental confusion, and coma. Treatment includes oxygen therapy and taking the person to a lower altitude. Because brain damage may be permanent, descent should begin as soon as cerebral edema is suspected (Hultgren, 1982). The best method for preventing HACE is a slow rate of ascent with adequate time for acclimatization.

Retinal Hemorrhage

Small hemorrhages may occur in the retina of the eye at altitudes above 3,600 m. The hemorrhage is thought to be due to increased blood flow and pressure in the retinal vessels (Kramar, Drinkwater, Folinsbee, & Bedi, 1983). Blood flow must increase to the retina to maintain an adequate supply of oxygen when at altitude. Often the hemorrhages are asymptomatic and disappear within a few weeks or months without any treatment. Occasionally the hemorrhage occurs in the macula, which may cause a blind spot in the central vision. Descent is advisable if hemorrhage occurs in the macula (Hultgren, 1982).

Other Medical Problems at Altitude

Because low temperatures are common at high altitudes, hypothermia and frostbite are common (see Chapter 3 for discussion of symptoms and treatment). Sunburn occurs frequently because of the increased ultraviolet radiation (UV-B) at altitude. Insomnia and periodic breathing (Cheyne-Stokes) may persist in some individuals who have difficulty acclimatizing to altitude (Hultgren, 1982). Chronic mountain sickness (Monge's disease) occurs in older altitude natives and is a result of polycythemia (hematocrit < 70%) and a depressed ventilatory response.

PERFORMANCE AT ALTITUDE

Distance Events

Before the 1968 Olympic Games at Mexico City investigators from several countries conducted research on the effects of altitude on performance. Most of the studies focused on performance in the endurance events of 1 mile or longer at 2,300 m. The results from several studies are presented in Table 4.3. Running time increased at altitude for all of the events longer than 440 yd. During the first week at 2,300 m, running time increased from 4% in the 880-yd run to 8.5% in the 3-mile run. Swimming times were slightly increased for the 100-yd events, with greater increases for the 200- and 500-yd events. At higher altitudes, running time increased for all events including a 13% increase in 440-yd at 4,000 m (Buskirk, Kollias, Akers, Prokop, & Picon-Reategui, 1967a).

Several investigators observed a reversal of finish order among athletes at altitude compared with sea level performances (Buskirk et al., 1967b; Pugh, 1967). Two possible reasons have been suggested for this. Both Pugh (1967a) and Saltin (1967) suggested that a small lung diffusion capacity might inhibit oxygen uptake in some athletes at altitude and explain their relatively poor performance. Saltin (1967) also suggested that differences in anaerobic capacity influence performance at altitude. Because $\dot{V}O_2$max is reduced at altitude, a person running at the same speed at altitude as at sea level uses less aerobic energy and more anaerobic energy. If the athlete has a small anaerobic capacity, running speed must decrease more than if the anaerobic capacity is large. The athlete with the largest anaerobic capacity has an advantage at altitude among competitors who are otherwise equally matched (Saltin, 1967).

Table 4.3

Reduction in Performance at Different Altitudes

Altitude (Study)	Event	Reduction in Performance
2,270 m (Pugh, 1967)	1 mile	3.6%
	3 mile	8.5%
2,300 m (Faulkner, 1967)	440 yd	1.0%
	880 yd	4.0%
	1 mile	6.0%
	2 mile	5.0%
	Swimming—100 yd	2.0%
	Swimming—200 yd	5.0%
	Swimming—500 yd	6.0%
3,100 m (Grover & Reeves, 1967)	220 yd	−7.5%
	440 yd	−5.5%
	880 yd	1.2%
	1 mile	7.5%
4,000 m (Buskirk et al., 1967a)	440 yd	13.4%
	880 yd	21.9%
	1 mile	30.4%
	2 mile	24.0%

Performance in the distance events at the 1968 Olympics in Mexico City was better than had been predicted from the decrement in $\dot{V}O_2$max (Craig & Dvorak, 1969. Keino's time in the 1,500-m race was only 0.8% slower than the world record, and his time for 5,000 m was only 6% slower than the world record. Keino as well as Temu, winner at 10,000 m, and Biwott, winner of the 3,000-m steeplechase, were from Kenya and had lived and trained at an altitude similar to that of Mexico City.

Pugh (1970) suggested that the reduction in air resistance caused by the lower air density at 2,270 m may account for the smaller decline in running times than was predicted from the decrement in $\dot{V}O_2$max. Barometric pressure is 23.5% lower in Mexico City than at sea level. Pugh calculated that 8% of the total energy used in running 5,000 m is needed to overcome air resistance at sea level. The reduction in air resistance at altitude is directly proportional to the reduction in air density and barometric pressure. This would reduce the net energy cost in the 5,000-m run by 1.9% (8.0 × 0.235), which approximates the difference between the decrement in winning time for the 5,000-m (6%) and an estimated 8% decrement in $\dot{V}O_2$max (Pugh, 1970).

Decreased air density and air resistance should also reduce the energy cost of distance races in cycling, speed skating, and cross-country skiing.

Sprinting Events

Improved performances were predicted for the running events lasting less than 2 min at Mexico City because of the reduction in air density and air resistance. Grover and Reeves (1967) reported sprinters had faster times for the 200- and 440-yd runs at 3,100 m than at sea level (see Table 4.3). New world record times were set in the 100-, 200-, and 400-m runs for men and the 100-, 200-, and 800-m runs for women in the 1968 Olympics (Stiles, 1969). The time for the men's 800-m run equaled the world record set at sea level. The world record time in the men's 400-m run still is the world record in 1985. The present 100-m record was set in Colorado Springs in 1983 and the 4 × 400 relay was not broken until the 1984 Olympics. Improvement in times for the men's 100- and 200-m dashes was 1% at 2,300 m, and the time of the 400-m run was 1.6% faster. Pugh (1970) estimated that 16% of the energy cost of running 100 m was used to overcome air resistance. The predicted reduction in energy cost would be 4% (16 × 0.235) at an altitude of 2,300 m. Apparently other factors influenced performance in the sprints at Mexico City in addition to reduced air resistance.

World record times were also achieved in several swimming events lasting 1 min or less at Mexico City. Slower times had been predicted in swimming events lasting 2 min or longer at Mexico City (Faulkner, 1967; Goddard & Favour, 1967). Because reduced air resistance should have little effect on swimming times, improvement in performance was most likely due to training. The decrement in several of the longer races was considerably less than predicted from the experimental studies conducted before the 1968 Olympics.

Lowered air resistance resulted in faster times in the cycling sprints at Mexico City compared with events at sea level. The reduction in air density at altitude should also reduce air resistance and increase speed in the alpine skiing (slalom, giant slalom, and downhill) and speed skating events.

Power Events

Because of the reduction in gravitational force and air resistance, some improvement in each of the throwing events was predicted for the 1968 Olympics in Mexico City. The smallest improvement over sea level performance (6 cm) was predicted for the shot, and the largest (162 cm) was predicted for the discus (Balke, 1967). However, only two world records for men were established in the field events at the 1968 Olympics—the long jump and pole vault. Bob Beamon's record in the long jump of 8.9 m deserves special mention because it still stood as the world record 17 years later in 1985. The decrease in air resistance should have increased the speed of take-off for the jump, while the decreased force of gravity should have slightly increased the time of flight. The world record in the triple jump was also set in Mexico City in 1975 and was not broken until 1985.

Muscular Strength and Endurance

Although hypoxia decreases $\dot{V}O_2max$, it seems that muscular endurance does not decrease at altitudes up to 4,600 m (Young, Wright, Knapik, & Cymerman, 1980). No significant decrement in either static or dynamic strength has been observed at 4,600 m compared with sea level. Acute mountain sickness, which develops during the first 24 hours at altitude, also appears to have little effect on muscular strength or endurance.

Training at Altitude

There are two strategies that sea level residents can use to perform at altitudes of 1,500 m and above. The first is to arrive at altitude within 12 hr of the performance. This strategy has been followed by many collegiate and professional athletic teams competing at sites in the Rocky Mountains. By performing during the first 12 hours at altitude, the athlete reduces the chance that acute mountain sickness will affect the performance.

The second strategy is to spend several weeks training at the same altitude before the performance. Several studies conducted before the 1968 Olympics strongly suggested that $\dot{V}O_2max$ and performance improved after training for several weeks at altitude (Buskirk et al., 1967b; Pugh, 1967; Saltin, 1967). This strategy has been adopted by many athletes preparing for competition at altitude. Training intensity must be reduced because $\dot{V}O_2max$ is lower at altitude than at sea level. By training at altitude, the athlete learns to adjust the exercise intensity accordingly. Two weeks is probably the minimum time an athlete should spend training at altitude for competition at altitude. During the first few days at altitude, athletes may experience acute mountain sickness, which may hinder their training.

RETURN TO SEA LEVEL

Does training at altitude improve performance at sea level? The outstanding performance of the Kenyan runners in the 1968 Olympics fueled speculation that long-term training at altitude might enhance performance in long-distance races at sea level as well as at altitude. If the athlete remained at altitude for several months, the increase in red blood cell volume would increase the oxygen content of the blood. Theoretically, this should be an advantage on returning to sea level, because oxygen transport would be increased.

Physiological Adjustments

When an altitude-acclimatized person returns to sea level, red blood cell volume decreases and plasma volume increases within the first 2 weeks (Reynafarje et al., 1959). Erythrocyte formation by the bone marrow is depressed by the end of the first week at sea level. When hemoglobin concentration decreases to sea level values, CaO_2 also returns to the prealtitude level, and any advantage gained in oxygen transport at altitude is lost. Two months after returning to sea level, total blood volume decreases and red blood cell volume may fall below normal. The decline in hemoglobin further reduces CaO_2.

Although a decrease in hemoglobin is a disadvantage in terms of oxygen transport, the reduction in hematocrit and viscosity reduces the resistance to blood flow. Stroke volume returns to normal sea level values and increases maximal cardiac output. During submaximal exercise, heart rate returns to a lower level than at altitude.

On returning to sea level the hypoxic stimulus is removed and the peripheral chemoreceptors no longer stimulate respiration, because PO_2 returns to normal (100 torr). Initially ventilation decreases, but this allows PCO_2 to increase above normal (< 40 torr). Because the CSF bicarbonate levels decreased at altitude, an increase in CSF CO_2 decreases the pH and stimulates the central chemoreceptors. Hyperventilation continues at sea level for several weeks until the CSF bicarbonate levels return to normal.

Performance

Several studies have reported no improvement in maximal oxygen uptake or performance in running events after several weeks of training at altitudes ranging from 2,300 to 4,000 m compared with prealtitude performance (Adams, Bernauer, Dill, & Bomar, 1975; Buskirk et al., 1967a; Faulkner, Kollias, Favour, Buskirk, & Balke, 1968). Performance and $\dot{V}O_2$max were measured during the first week after returning to sea level, which theoretically should be before hemoglobin concentration returns to sea level values. When runners native to 3,100 m perform at sea level, their performance was no better than that of sea level natives (Grover & Reeves, 1967). On the other hand, when 2-week training periods at 2,300 m were separated by a few days of training at sea level, postaltitude $\dot{V}O_2$max improved by 5% (Daniels & Oldridge, 1970). Improvement in $\dot{V}O_2$max is more likely in persons who were relatively untrained before altitude training than in highly trained athletes (Kollias & Buskirk, 1974).

One disadvantage of training at altitude is that exercise intensity must be reduced. At 4,000 m the training intensity had to be reduced to 40% of the sea level intensity for the first 3 weeks (Buskirk et al., 1967a). Duration and intensity gradually increased over the 8 weeks at altitude to 75% of the sea level training. To decrease exercise intensity, the runner and cross-country skier must slow their pace. On returning to sea level, this could be a disadvantage in a race—particularly when competing against athletes who have been training at sea level at a faster pace. To overcome this obstacle, the athlete would have to train at a higher percentage of $\dot{V}O_2$max. The middle distance runners studied by Daniels and Oldridge (1970) were able to maintain a pace for 3 miles that was approximately the same at 2,300 m as at sea level.

The increased red blood cell volume of altitude can be experimentally reproduced by removing two units of blood (approximately 900 ml) from a person, freezing the red blood cells, and then reinfusing the cells 6 weeks later. Using this technique to induce erythrocythemia, several studies have reported improvements in $\dot{V}O_2$max and performance 24 hours after the red blood cells were reinfused (Buick, Gledhill, Froese, & Spriet, 1982; Robertson, et al., 1982; Williams, Wesseldine, Somma, & Schuster, 1981). The percentage increase in $\dot{V}O_2$max was less than the increase in hemoglobin concentration and the improvement in endurance. Robertson et al. (1982) found that this technique improved performance during hypoxia as well as at sea level. The results suggest that improved performances could be expected during the first 24 hours at sea level and probably longer.

SUMMARY

Because of the decline in barometric pressure as altitude increases, the P_IO_2 also decreases. A reduction in P_IO_2 decreases the amount of oxygen transported by the blood. To compensate for the reduction in available oxygen, hemoglobin concentration and ventilation increase. The initial increase in hemoglobin is due to a loss of plasma volume. Increasing ventilation elevates the amount of oxygen present in the alveoli and facilitates diffusion into the blood. An increase in hemoglobin content increases the amount of oxygen in the blood.

To supply the same amount of oxygen to the tissues during submaximal exercise, the heart rate is greater at altitude than at sea level. Because maximal heart rate at altitude is unlikely to increase, $\dot{V}O_2$max is reduced. Performance in endurance activities lasting more than 2 minutes is reduced at altitudes of 2,300 m and above. However, performance in sprinting events is likely to improve because of the reduction in air density at altitude.

Acclimatization to altitude includes an increase in red blood cell volume after several months' residence. High-altitude natives have larger lung diffusion capacities and greater blood flow through the pulmonary capillaries than sea level natives. These adaptations facilitate the transfer of oxygen from the air to the blood and increase the arterial oxygen content.

On returning to sea level, hemoglobin concentration decreases during the first several weeks. Any improvement in endurance performance at sea level occurs while the hemoglobin content is elevated.

Rapid ascent to altitudes of 2,100 m and above increases the risk of altitude illness. Acute mountain sickness can be prevented by reducing the rate of ascent, increasing the intake of fluids and carbohydrates, and by taking acetazolamide the day before a rapid ascent and the first day at altitude. High-altitude pulmonary edema (HAPE) and cerebral edema (HACE) occur at higher altitudes and are less common than AMS. Both are extremely serious and require medical treatment and moving the person to a lower altitude.

Athletes who are going to compete at altitudes of 2,300 m and above should plan to spend 2 to 3 weeks acclimatizing to the altitude before competition. Some improvement in performance at altitude is seen with acclimatization.

5

Air Pollution
and Performance

This chapter provides an overview of the effects of air pollution on exercise. We begin by examining the different types of air pollutants and their sources. Next we examine the physiological responses to each of the pollutants. The body responds to various pollutants in different ways. Some pollutants, such as ozone and sulfur dioxide, irritate the respiratory tract, whereas carbon monoxide takes the place of oxygen in the blood. Next we examine whether there is a lower threshold for some or all of the pollutants during exercise.

During air pollution episodes, two or more pollutants are likely to be elevated simultaneously. We will examine how the body responds when two pollutants are present at the same time. We will also discuss the interaction between the environment and pollutants. Photochemical smog usually occurs during warm weather, so we will examine whether the exercise responses are due to the heat, the pollutants, or both.

Finally, we will examine how air pollutants affect sports performance. Although much interest has been directed toward the effects of smog at the 1984 Olympics in Los Angeles, athletes performing in many other metropolitan areas may also be affected by air pollutants.

We will discuss the following questions in this chapter:

- What is an acceptable level of the pollutant in the environment, and what levels are causes for concern?
- Is there a threshold level for each pollutant?
- Is there a lower threshold for some or all of the pollutants during exercise?

- Are athletes more likely to be affected by air pollution than sedentary persons?
- Are the exercise responses due to the heat, the pollutants, or both?

AIR POLLUTANTS

Pollutants are foreign substances that change the quality of the environment. Although air pollutants are usually thought to be by-products of the industrial revolution, many pollutants are produced by natural sources. For example, volcanoes emit sulfur oxides and ash (particulate matter) into the atmosphere, and lightning produces ozone. There are two main classifications of air pollutants. Primary pollutants are produced directly and include carbon monoxide (CO), sulfur oxides (SO_x), nitrogen oxides (NO_x), hydrocarbons, and particulates. Secondary pollutants are produced by interactions between primary pollutants and the environment and include ozone (O_3), peroxyacetyl nitrate (PAN), aldehydes, sulfuric acid (H_2SO_4), and sulfates. The smog or brown cloud that is associated with many metropolitan areas usually contains both primary and secondary pollutants.

Primary Pollutants

Carbon monoxide is produced by the incomplete combustion of organic materials including gasoline, oil, wood, and tobacco. The automobile is the major source of carbon monoxide in the atmosphere. In enclosed environments, smoking is the main source of carbon monoxide. Sulfur oxides are produced by burning sulfur-containing fuels such as coal and oil. Sulfur dioxide (SO_2) is the main pollutant in this group. Much of the sulfur dioxide comes from industrial sources and power plants.

Nitrogen oxides are emitted by automobiles, aircraft, industrial sources, and burning coal and oil. Several forms of nitrogen oxides are produced, but "nitrogen dioxide causes the most concern because of its toxicity and concentration in urban smog" (Henschel, 1974, p. 481). Hydrocarbons are also released into the atmosphere from automobile exhaust.

Particulate matter includes dust, smoke, ash, and aerosols. Industry and transportation vehicles are the major sources of particulate matter in the urban atmosphere. Natural sources that also contribute particulates to the atmosphere are forest fires, dust storms, and volcano eruptions. The eruption of Mt. St. Helens in 1980 deposited a large amount of particulate matter across the northern half of the United States.

Secondary Pollutants

The photochemical reaction of nitrogen dioxide (NO_2) and hydrocarbons in the presence of sunlight produces most ozone, the most hazardous pollutant. Ozone is also produced naturally by lightning. Although ozone is dangerous in the atmosphere, a layer of ozone in the stratosphere helps protect the earth from most destructive ultraviolet rays. Small amounts of ozone are also produced by electrical equipment that produces sparks or electrical arcs. Peroxyacetyl nitrate is also produced by the same photochemical reaction between CO_2 and hydrocarbons. Ozone and PAN form what is known as photochemical smog.

In the presence of other air pollutants and sunlight sulfur dioxide is oxidized to form sulfur trioxide (SO_3). Sulfur trioxide immediately reacts with any water vapor in the atmosphere to form sulfuric acid,

$$SO_3 + H_2O = H_2SO_4.$$

Sulfuric acid then reacts with particulates to form sulfates. Sulfuric acid is a more hazardous pollutant than sulfur dioxide and is often referred to as acid rain. This type of smog, known as London-type smog, is produced when the humidity is high and the temperature is low.

Air Quality Standards

Smog is a common problem in many metropolitan areas throughout the world. Several air pollution episodes during the past 50 years have increased the rate of death from respiratory diseases. These include incidents in the Meuse Valley of Belgium in 1930; Donora, Pennsylvania in 1948; and London in 1952. To reduce the risk of such incidents, the United States established air quality standards for six pollutants in 1971. The most recent revision of these standards is presented in Table 5.1. Primary air quality standards are defined as those "necessary, with an adequate margin of safety, to protect the public health" (Office of the Federal Register, 1983, pp. 563-564). The secondary standards are those needed to protect the public welfare. Pollutant quantities are expressed in either parts per million (ppm) or micrograms per cubic meter of air ($\mu g \cdot m^{-3}$).

When the concentration of one or more of the pollutants rises above the primary standard, a second set of emergency criteria is used to evaluate the health risk. These are presented in Table 5.2. The Environmental Protection Agency has recently adopted a numerical Pollutant Standards Index (PSI) that corresponds to the emergency criteria. A PSI value of 100 was set to corres-

Table 5.1

Primary and Secondary Air Quality Standards

Pollutant	Primary Standard	Secondary Standard
Ozone	0.12 ppm 1 hr avg.	0.12 ppm 1 hr avg.
Carbon monoxide	9.0 ppm 8 hr avg.	9.0 ppm 8 hr avg.
	35.0 ppm 1 hr avg.	35.0 ppm 1 hr avg.
Nitrogen dioxide	0.05 ppm AAM*	0.05 ppm AAM
Sulfur dioxide	0.14 ppm 24 hr avg.	0.50 ppm 3 hr avg.
Particulate matter	260 μg·m^{-3} 24 hr avg.	150 μg·m^{-3} 24 hr avg.
Hydrocarbons	0.24 ppm 3 hr avg.	0.24 ppm 3 hr avg.
Lead	1.5 μg·m^{-3} AAM*	1.5 μg·m^{-3} AAM

*AAM = annual arithmetric mean

pond with the primary standard for five of the pollutants: carbon monoxide, ozone, sulfur dioxide, nitrogen dioxide, and total particulates. PSI values between 100 and 200 are considered unhealthy, between 200 and 300 are very unhealthy, and above 300 are hazardous to health. Data collected from 43 cities in 1976 indicated that a PSI value of greater than 100 occurred at least 50% of the year in Los Angeles, Denver, Cleveland, and St. Louis (McCafferty, 1981).

Smog Formation

Why does smog form in some metropolitan areas but not in others? In addition to the pollutants generated in a particular area, several other factors, including weather conditions, wind speed and direction, and the geography of the region, help determine whether smog is likely to be produced. Photochemical smog (the type in Los Angeles) is produced when the weather is warm and there is an abundance of sunshine to help oxidize oxygen to ozone.

Table 5.2

Emergency Criteria and Air Pollutant Concentrations

Pollutant	Alert Level	Warning Level	Emergency Action	Significant Harm to Health
Ozone	.10 ppm 1 hr avg.	.40 ppm 1 hr avg.	.50 ppm 1 hr avg.	.60 ppm 1 hr avg.
Carbon monoxide	15 ppm 8 hr avg.	30 ppm 8 hr avg.	40 ppm 8 hr avg.	50 ppm 8 hr avg.
Nitrogen dioxide	.15 ppm 24 hr avg.	.30 ppm 24 hr avg.	.40 ppm 24 hr avg.	.50 ppm 24 hr avg.
	.60 ppm 1 hr avg.	1.2 ppm 1 hr avg.	1.6 ppm 1 hr avg.	2.0 ppm 1 hr avg.
Sulfur dioxide	.30 ppm 24 hr avg.	.60 ppm 24 hr avg.	.80 ppm 24 hr avg.	1.0 ppm 24 hr avg.
Particulates	375 $\mu g \cdot m^{-3}$ 24 hr avg.	625 $\mu g \cdot m^{-3}$ 24 hr avg.	875 $\mu g \cdot m^{-3}$ 24 hr avg.	1,000 $\mu g \cdot m^{-3}$ 24 hr avg.
PSI value	200	300	400	500

Temperature inversions prevent the pollutants from rising more than a few hundred feet above the ground. Under normal circumstances, air that is next to the ground is warmed and rises to be replaced by cooler air. In a temperature inversion, a layer of cool air next to the ground is trapped by a layer of warmer air above it. When there is very little wind to disperse the pollutants and break the temperature inversion, a favorable set of conditions exists for smog formation.

The topography of a region also influences smog formation. Mountain and river valleys are likely to have smog problems if sufficient amounts of air pollutants are emitted into the atmosphere. If the prevailing wind direction is toward the mountains, the pollutants will be trapped against the mountain barrier. This is the case in Los Angeles during the summer when the prevailing wind is from the Pacific Ocean and blows the pollutants toward the mountain ranges to the north and east. A similar situation occurs in Denver when the wind is from the east, which traps the pollutants against the Rocky Mountains. The result is a brown cloud covering the Denver metropolitan area.

London-type smog is most likely to be produced during the winter, when the air temperature is low. During cold weather the burning of coal and oil to heat homes and businesses increases the amount of sulfur dioxide in the atmosphere. In the presence of particulate matter and high humidity, part of the sulfur dioxide is converted to sulfuric acid and sulfates. If there is little air movement, the pollutants remain stationary over an area and their concentration increases. Such was the case for 4 days in London during December, 1952. It is estimated that 4,000 deaths from respiratory diseases occurred during this air pollution incident (McCafferty, 1981). Similar smog episodes have occurred in the Meuse Valley (Belgium) and Donora, Pennsylvania.

Geographical Distribution

Many metropolitan areas across the United States reported violations of the primary standard for one or more of the pollutants during the 1970s. Violations of the primary 8-hour standard for CO (9 ppm) were reported by 72% of the CO-monitoring sites that were operating in 1973 (see Figure 5.1). By 1977 the percentage of sites reporting violations had dropped to 46% (Environmental Criteria and Assessment Office, 1979). This trend toward fewer violations was also observed in Los Angeles and Denver, two cities that report frequent violations of the 8-hour standard. Denver reported 152 violations in 1972 but only 48 in 1977. The number of violations in Los Angeles decreased

Figure 5.1. Carbon monoxide levels in the United States, 1973.

Note. From the U.S. Environmental Protection Agency.

from 172 in 1968 to 64 in 1977. The reduction in CO violations is believed to be due to air pollution controls on newer automobiles.

The primary standard for ozone (0.08 ppm) is violated in many metropolitan areas across the United States. Los Angeles has the highest oxidant concentrations and the most frequent violations (Office of Research and Development, 1978). Most of the cities in the Washington, DC to Boston corridor report high oxidant concentrations. Denver, Houston, and St. Louis also report frequent violations of the oxidant standard and elevated concentrations.

Elevated SO_2 levels are most often found near smelters, steel mills, and paper mills (Environmental Criteria and Assement Office, 1982). The cities that report the highest 24-hour levels are in the Northeast (Philadelphia, Pittsburgh, and New York) and Midwest (Toledo and Hammond, Indiana). More than 100 cities and counties reported 1-hour SO_2 exceeding 0.4 ppm during the past few years. The highest sulfate levels, averaging more than 15 $\mu g \cdot m^{-3}$, are found in the Ohio Valley. Most of the states east of the Mississippi River have annual average sulfate levels exceeding 10 $\mu g \cdot m^{-3}$ with the exception of upper New England and the South Atlantic area.

PHYSIOLOGICAL RESPONSES TO THE POLLUTANTS

Carbon Monoxide

When carbon monoxide is present in the air we breathe, some of it combines with hemoglobin to form carboxyhemoglobin (COHb). The CO molecule takes the place of an oxygen molecule bound to iron and reduces the oxygen content of the blood. Hemoglobin's affinity for CO is 210 times greater than for oxygen. How much CO enters the blood is determined by the CO content of the air, alveolar ventilation, diffusion capacity of the lung, and the hemoglobin content (Horvath, 1982). Duration of exposure to CO also determines how much of the hemoglobin combines with CO. Table 5.3 illustrates the increase in COHb level as exposure time increases (Peterson & Stewart, 1970).

Because CO takes the place of oxygen, the arterial oxygen content decreases as the COHb level increases. If the blood contains 5% COHb, arterial saturation with oxygen (SaO_2) decreases from 96% to 91%. Assuming a hemoglobin concentration of 15 $gm \cdot dl^{-1}$, a 5% COHb level would reduce the arterial oxygen content (CaO_2) from 19.3 ml $O_2 \cdot dl^{-1}$ to 18.3 ml $\cdot dl^{-1}$. If the same amount of oxygen is used at the tissue level with or without CO, either the venous oxygen content will be reduced by the same amount (1 ml $\cdot dl^{-1}$), or cardiac output ($\dot{Q}$) will have to increase. At rest $\dot{V}O_2$ is maintained during CO exposures up to 20% COHb by reducing the venous oxen content rather than by increasing heart rate or stroke volume (Vogel & Gleser, 1972).

The binding of CO to hemoglobin increases the affinity of the hemoglobin to oxygen. In other words, the hemoglobin gives up less oxygen at a given

Table 5.3

Exposure to CO and COHb Levels for Varying Lengths of Time

CO (ppm)	Time (min)	COHb (%)
50	30	1.3
	60	2.1
	180	3.8
	360	5.1
100	30	2.0
	60	3.3
	120	4.0
	180	6.4
	240	7.3
	480	12.4

Note. From Absorption and elimination of carbon monoxide by inactive young men (p. 166-167) by J.E. Peterson and R.D. Stewart, 1970, *Archives of Environmental Health*, **21**. Reprinted with permission.

tissue PO_2 when the COHb level increases. This is the equivalent of shifting the oxygen dissociation curve to the left (see Figure 5.2). For the same amount of oxygen to be unloaded in the tissues, the tissue PO_2 will have to be reduced even further. For most organs and tissues this is not a problem, because they extract only 25% of the oxygen in the blood at rest. However, cardiac muscle extracts 60% to 70% of the oxygen in the coronary blood (Comroe, 1974). Elevated COHb levels may prevent cardiac muscle from receiving enough oxygen.

Carbon monoxide is odorless, which makes it difficult to detect without monitoring equipment. Its accumulation in the blood also is not detected by the chemoreceptors, which allows it to reach a lethal level without any warning. When the COHb level rises, the chemoreceptors in the carotid and aortic bodies are not stimulated by the decrease in oxygen content. Because there is no change in the amount of oxygen dissolved in the plasma when CO is present in the blood, the PO_2 of the blood remains constant. The chemoreceptors are stimulated by a decrease in PO_2 or dissolved oxygen but are not affected by changes in hemoglobin saturation with oxygen. Increasing CO levels do not stimulate ventilation to increase. Therefore, the victim of carbon monoxide poisoning is unaware of impending disaster. Headache and nausea are symptoms when the COHb level exceeds 20%, and this may be the only warning to a person exposed to a toxic buildup of CO in an enclosed environment. Convulsions and coma occur at COHb levels above 50%, and 70% to 80% COHb levels are usually fatal (Horvath, 1982).

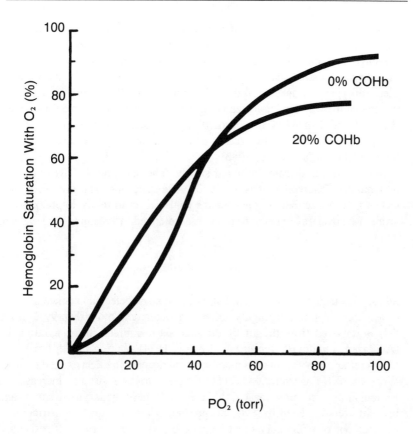

Figure 5.2. Relationship between hemoglobin saturation with O_2 and PO_2 for human blood containing 0% and 20% COHb.

Note. From "The effect of carbon monoxide on the oxyhemoglobin dissociation curve," by F.J.W. Roughton & R.C. Darling, 1944, *American Journal of Physiology*, **141**, 28. Adapted with permission.

The COHb level of nonsmokers breathing fresh air is less than 1%. A small amount of CO is produced endogenously during the normal destruction of hemoglobin at the end of the red blood cells' lifespan, which results in a 0.4% to 0.5% COHb level. The COHb level of cigarette smokers increases in direct proportion to the number of cigarettes smoked, and smokers who inhale have slightly higher levels than those who do not inhale (Goldsmith & Landaw, 1968). Light smokers (10 cigarettes or less per day) average approximately 4% COHb, while heavy smokers (2 packs or more) average about 7% COHb. Passive smoking is a significant source of CO that many nonsmokers are exposed to in enclosed buildings and cars. Peak CO levels may reach 90 ppm in poorly ventilated areas. Exposure to 90 ppm CO for 1 hour would result in a 3% COHb level (Peterson & Stewart, 1970). Such an exposure could occur traveling in a car with a smoker.

Motor vehicle exhaust is the major source of CO in the environment. Peak CO levels occur during the morning and evening rush hours. Both drivers and passengers of automobiles as well as pedestrians, joggers, and persons working adjacent to streets and highways are exposed to CO levels that may exceed 100 ppm during peak traffic (Haagen-Smith, 1966). For example, 90 minutes of freeway driving increased the COHb level from 1% to 5% (Aronow, Harris, Isbell, Rokaw, & Imparato, 1972). Elevated COHb levels (4% to 5% COHb) have also been observed in pedestrians and joggers during the rush hour (Nicholson and Case, 1983).

CO is eliminated from the blood slowly. The half-life of COHb averages 320 minutes (Peterson & Stewart, 1970). After a 60-min exposure to 100 ppm CO, it takes more than 8 hours for the COHb level to return to preexposure levels. Removal of CO from the blood is accelerated by breathing pure oxygen.

Sulfur Dioxide

Sulfur dioxide is a colorless gas, but its odor can be detected in concentrations of less than 1 ppm. It is highly soluble in water, and more than 99% of the SO_2 is removed from the air by the mucous membrane in the nasal cavity (Andersen, Lundqvist, Jensen, & Proctor, 1974). During mouth breathing, SO_2 is removed by the mucous membranes in the pharynx, larynx, and trachea. When the SO_2 concentration reaches 5 ppm, airway resistance increases. It is thought that receptors located in the epithelium of the larynx, trachea, and bronchi are stimulated by SO_2 and produce a reflex bronchoconstriction.

A number of pulmonary function tests are used to determine if resistance to air flow has increased. These include airway resistance measured in a body plethysmograph; maximal breathing capacity (MBC), which is also known as maximal voluntary ventilation (MVV); forced expiratory volume in 1 second (FEV_1); forced expiratory volume as a percent of the forced vital capacity (FEV/FVC); forced expiratory flow during the middle of the expired volume ($FEF_{25-75\%}$) and at 50% FEV (FEF_{50}) and 75% FEV (FEF_{75}); functional residual capacity (FRC); and closing volume tests. Decreases in FEV_1, FEV/FVC, and $FEF_{25-75\%}$ are thought to be good indicators of increased resistance to air flow in the large airways, while increased closing volume and $FEF_{75\%}$ are thought to indicate narrowing of the small airways (Folinsbee, Horvath, Bedi, & Delehunt, 1978; Folinsbee, et al., 1977; Koenig, Pierson, & Frank, 1980).

Asthmatic persons are more sensitive to SO_2 than average individuals. Increased airway resistance is observed at a SO_2 concentration of 1 ppm in asthmatic subjects after 10 minutes exposure but in normal subjects only at 5 ppm and above (Sheppard, Wong, Uehara, Nadel, & Boushey, 1980). However, after several hours' exposure to 1 ppm SO_2, increased airway resistance and decreased $FEF_{25-75\%}$ and FEV_1 are seen in normal persons (Andersen et al., 1974). The increase in resistance appears to be due to bronchoconstriction of the larger airways (trachea and bronchi), because no change in closing volume was observed. Mucus flow in the nasal cavity is depressed when a person is exposed to 5 ppm SO_2 for several hours.

Particulates

Particulate matter, including dust, smoke, and aerosols, is frequently present in the air we breathe. Large particles (diameter $< 10 \mu$) are filtered out of the air as it passes through the nasal cavity, pharynx and larynx (Comroe, 1974). Somewhat smaller particles (2 to 10 μ) are removed in the trachea and bronchi. All of these particles are removed from the large airways either forcefully by sneezing or coughing or slowly by the beating of the cilia that line the walls of the respiratory tract. The beating of the cilia, which resembles the stroking of oars, moves a layer of mucus upward toward the nose. Particles with diameters between 0.3 and 2 μ are most likely to reach the small air passages and be deposited in the alveoli. Macrophages located in the alveoli are responsible for digesting particles before they can damage the alveolar tissue. These macrophages are then removed from the respiratory tract by migrating to the mucus layer, where they are propelled to the large airways by the cilia. Very small particles (diameter $> 0.3 \mu$) are likely to remain as aerosols in the exhaled air.

Irritation of the large airways by particulates stimulates reflex coughing and bronchoconstriction. The stimulus necessary to produce bronchoconstriction is less than that needed for coughing. Because bronchoconstriction increases airway resistance, some changes in pulmonary function might be expected when breathing air containing particulates. However, breathing a sodium chloride (NaCl) aerosol with a mean diameter of 0.9 μ and at concentrations up to 1 mg•m^{-3} appears to have little effect on pulmonary function (Koenig et al., 1980; Sackner et al., 1978).

Sulfur dioxide can be adsorbed onto aerosol droplets, or in the presence of sunlight, it can be converted to H_2SO_4 or a sulfate aerosol. Sulfuric acid aerosols with concentrations up to 1 mg•m^{-3} do not affect pulmonary function (Sackner et al., 1978; Lippmann, Albert, Yeates, Wales, & Leikauf, 1980). However, H_2SO_4 (1 mg/m^3) reduces the clearance of mucus from the small airways (Lippmann et al., 1980). Breathing a 1 ppm SO_2 + 1 mg•m^{-3} NaCl aerosol decreased FEV_1 in healthy adolescents (Koenig et al., 1982) and maximal flow at 50% and 75% FEV in asthmatics (Koenig et al., 1980).

Nitrogen Dioxide

Of the different forms of nitrogen oxides in the atmosphere, nitrogen dioxide (NO_2) causes the most concern. At concentrations of 10 ppm NO_2 produces pulmonary edema. Chronic exposure of rats to 3 ppm NO_2 changes the surfactant of the alveoli and allows surface tension at the air-alveolar interface to increase (Arner & Rhoades, 1973). An increase in surface tension in the alveoli would require increased air pressure to inflate the lungs to a normal volume. Airway resistance increases when NO_2 exceeds 1.6 ppm (Horvath, 1982).

Under normal circumstances, the atmosphere does not contain NO_2 concentrations exceeding 1 ppm, but people in certain occupations (e.g., welding, fire fighting, silo filling) may experience higher concentrations. Exposure to 0.6 ppm NO_2 for 2 hours had little effect on pulmonary, metabolic, or cardiovascular function (Folinsbee, Horvath, et al., 1978). This level of NO_2 (0.6 ppm) is commonly observed in heavy smog. Because NO_2 is soluble, it is removed in the nasal cavity and pharynx by the mucous membranes. This will reduce the quantity of NO_2 that reaches the alveoli.

Ozone

Ozone is a secondary product of photochemical smog. It is considered to be the most dangerous of the gaseous pollutants. Most of the ozone that is inhaled remains in the respiratory tract, because little is found in the exhaled air. The amount of ozone taken up by the mucous membrane depends on the concentration gradient between the air and respiratory tissue. At higher concentrations more ozone penetrates the mucous membrane than at lower concentrations (Melton, 1982). Symptoms characteristic of ozone exposure include cough, substernal pain, throat irritation, inability to take a deep breath, and nausea.

Changes in several pulmonary function tests (FVC, FEV_1, $FEF_{25-75\%}$) are observed when the concentration of ozone exceeds 0.3 ppm. These changes are more likely in persons who are not habitually exposed to elevated ozone levels than in persons who live in areas with high oxidant air pollution (Hackney, Linn, Karuza, et al., 1977). The exact cause of the decreases in FEV_1, FVC, and $FEF_{25-75\%}$ is unknown, but bronchoconstriction is unlikely because there is very little increase in airway resistance (Hackney, Linn, Mohler & Collier, 1977b).

Repeated exposures to ozone result in a greater decrement in pulmonary function measures on the second day of exposure and an improvement in response by the third day (Folinsbee, Bedi, & Horvath, 1980; Hackney, Linn, Mohler, et al., 1977b). Ozone concentrations below the threshold level do not appear to produce a cumulative effect over a 3-day exposure period (Folinsbee et al., 1980). It has been suggested that irritant receptors in the respiratory tract increase in sensitivity on the second day because of epithelial tissue damage. Adaptation to ozone takes place over a 3- to 4-day period, with increased concentrations requiring a longer time than threshold levels. The exact mechanism involved in adaptation is unknown.

Ozone toxicity is thought to be due to its ability to produce free radicals (Melton, 1982). When ozone breaks down, it produces an oxygen molecule and an oxygen singlet, which accepts electrons because the outer shell is not completely filled with electrons. Other chemical compounds donate electrons to the oxygen singlet and in turn become free radicals. Double bonds between carbon atoms are especially vulnerable to peroxidation by the oxygen singlet. Lipids containing unsaturated fatty acids (one or more double bonds) are found in all cell membranes. The epithelial tissue that lines the respiratory tract is composed of densely packed cells. If the unsaturated fatty acids in the cell membrane are oxidized, the cell may be damaged.

Peroxyacetyl Nitrate

Another secondary product of photochemical oxidation is peroxyacetyl nitrate (PAN). PAN's concentration in the atmosphere rarely exceeds 0.1 ppm. It represents less than 1% of the total oxidants. The main effect of PAN appears to be to irritate the eyes (Gliner, Raven, Horvath, Drinkwater, & Sutton, 1975). Other symptoms of PAN include blurred vision and eye fatigue.

EXERCISE AND AIR POLLUTANTS

Carbon Monoxide

Theoretically, any increase in the COHb level should have an effect on the physiological responses to exercise. The accompanying reduction in the CaO_2 reduces the amount of oxygen available to the tissues. During submaximal exercise, the $\dot{V}O_2$ increases by increasing cardiac output and increasing the amount of oxygen extracted from the blood as it passes through the tissues ($a-\bar{v}O_2$ difference). Because both arterial and venous O_2 content decrease as the COHb level increases, most of the increase in $\dot{V}O_2$ is due to an increase in cardiac output, which in turn is due to an increased heart rate (Ekblom, Huot, Stein, & Thorstensson, 1975; Pirnay, Dujardin, Deroanne, & Petit, 1971; Vogel & Gleser, 1972). Arterial lactate levels increase during heavy exercise, which suggests that the relative exercise intensity increases as the COHb level increases (Vogel & Gleser, 1972).

Maximal oxygen intake is reduced when the COHb level exceeds 4.3% (Ekblom et al., 1975; Horvath, Raven, Dahms, & Gray, 1975; Pirnay et al., 1971; Vogel & Gleser, 1972). The decrement in $\dot{V}O_2$max appears to be linear above this point (see Figure 5.3). Because CO has replaced some of the O_2 bound to hemoglobin, the maximal $a-\bar{v}O_2$ differences are reduced, and maximal cardiac output cannot increase to compensate for the reduced oxygen ex-

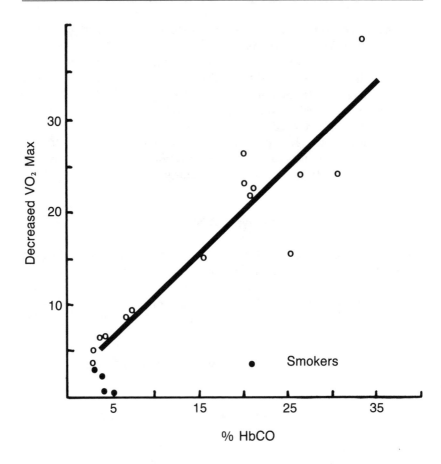

Figure 5.3. Relationship between HbCO and decrement in maximum aerobic power.

Note. From Impact of air quality on exercise performance (p. 288) by S.M. Horvath, 1982. In D.I. Miller (Ed.) *Exercise and Sport Sciences Reviews*, Philadelphia: The Franklin Institute. Reprinted with permission.

traction. The length of time a person can exercise is also reduced by elevated COHb levels (Horvath et al., 1975). Below 4% COHb there appears to be little effect on V̇O₂max and exercise time (Raven et al., 1974).

Runners who train on heavily traveled streets during rush hour are likely to have COHb levels that exceed 4% (Nicholson & Case, 1983). The uptake of CO by the blood during exercise may be accelerated by increases in alveolar ventilation and diffusion capacity, because the COHb level of nonrunners only reached 2% over the same time period. Exercise in relatively clean air may accelerate the removal of CO from the blood of smokers and nonsmokers (Horvath, 1982). There is less of an increase in COHb levels during exposure to 50 to 100 ppm CO in smokers than nonsmokers. Because smokers have higher COHb levels, the CO gradient between their lungs and blood is small compared with that of nonsmokers.

Sulfur Dioxide

Exercise increases the bronchoconstriction in asthmatic persons exposed to SO_2 (Koenig, Pierson, Horike, & Frank, 1981; Sheppard, Saisho, Nadel, & Boushey, 1981). Ventilation increases during exercise, which increases the amount of pollutant entering the air passageways. In addition, breathing occurs primarily through the mouth instead of the nose, bypassing the effective scrubbing action of the nasal mucosa. This allows more of the SO_2 to reach the trachea and bronchi. Airway resistance increases significantly during 10 minutes of exercise when asthmatics breathe 0.5 ppm SO_2 (Sheppard et al., 1981). Some asthmatics were affected by 0.25 ppm SO_2.

Healthy persons appear to be less sensitive to SO_2 during exercise than asthmatics (Koenig, Pierson, Horike, & Frank, 1982). Exposure to 0.4 ppm SO_2 during exercise has little effect on pulmonary function (Bedi, Folinsbee, Horvath, & Ebenstein, 1979). However, exposure to 1.0 ppm SO_2 during 10 minutes of moderate exercise reduces FEV_1 in healthy adolescents (Koenig et al., 1982). This suggests that the threshold for SO_2 for nonasthmatic persons during exercise is between 0.4 and 1.0 ppm. The decrease in FEV_1 was not as large in the healthy adolescents as in asthmatic adolescents.

Particulates

There have been few studies of the effects of particulates on the responses to exercise. Because ventilation increases during exercise, a greater volume of particulates enters the lungs. The switch from nasal to oral breathing during exercise also means that fewer particulates are removed in the nasal cavity than at rest. Ten minutes of exercise during exposure to a NaCl aerosol (1 mg•m^{-3}) had little effect on either airway resistance or pulmonary function (Koenig et al., 1982). However, the addition of 1 ppm SO_2 to the aerosol resulted in significant decreases in FEV_1 and $FEF_{50\%}$ and a 10% increase in FRC in healthy adolescents. The results of the pulmonary function tests suggest that more of the SO_2 + NaCl aerosol penetrated the small airways during exercise than at rest. Larger changes in FEV_1 and $FEF_{50\%}$ and an increase in airway resistance were observed in asthmatic adolescents during exercise after exposure to the SO_2 + NaCl aerosol than in the healthy adolescents (Koenig et al., 1981).

Nitrogen Dioxide

Intermittent exercise during exposure to NO_2 concentrations of 1 ppm or less has little effect on pulmonary function (Folinsbee, Horvath, et al., 1978; Hackney, Linn, Buckley, Collier, & Mohler, 1978). Because ambient NO_2 concentration rarely exceeds 1 ppm, most persons would not be exposed to higher levels during exercise. Unfortunately, it appears that there have been no studies in which the subjects exercised continuously for longer than 30 minutes or the exercise intensity exceeded 45% $\dot{V}O_2$max. At higher exercise intensities ventilation will be greater and more of the pollutant will be inhaled than at lower exercise intensities. The effects of exercise during exposure to NO_2 have not been studied in persons who may be more susceptible to NO_2 than normal (e.g., asthmatics).

Ozone

The volume of ozone inhaled increases during exercise because ventilation increases. In addition, because persons exercising at moderate and heavy intensities breathe through the mouth, any effect the nose has in removing ozone is bypassed. It has been suggested that the effect of ozone on pulmonary function can best be described by the effective dose of ozone, which is the product of ozone concentration times ventilation times exposure duration (Silverman, Folinsbee, Barnard, & Shephard, 1976). This suggests that for a particular ozone concentration (i.e., 0.3 ppm) a person exercising with a $\dot{V}_E$ of 60 L•min^{-1} would experience a greater change in pulmonary function measures than a person exercising for the same length of time with a $\dot{V}_E$ of 30 L•min^{-1}. There is a threshold for ozone of 0.3 ppm at 65% $\dot{V}O_2$max, which suggests that ozone concentration is the most important factor determining the response of the respiratory system (Adams, Savin, & Christo, 1981). During exercise at 75% $\dot{V}O_2$max, exposure to 0.2 ppm ozone decreases several pulmonary function tests (Bedi, Folinsbee, & Horvath, 1983).

Pulmonary function changes include decreases in FVC, FEV_1, $FEF_{25-75\%}$, and MVV after exercise while breathing ozone (Folinsbee, Drinkwater, Bedi, & Horvath, 1978). The decrease in FVC is primarily due to a decrease in inspiratory capacity. Tidal volume decreases during exercise while breathing ozone. However, $\dot{V}_E$ is maintained by increasing respiratory frequency. Ozone exposure during maximal exercise results in a decrease in $\dot{V}_E$max (Folinsbee, Silverman, & Shephard, 1977; Savin & Adams, 1979). Reduced $\dot{V}_E$max is accompanied by a reduction in tidal volume with no reduction in maximal respiratory frequency (Folinsbee et al., 1977). The decrease in tidal volume during exercise while breathing ozone is thought to be due to the decreased inspiratory capacity.

Maximal oxygen uptake is only slightly decreased (3%) during exposure to 0.3 ppm ozone (Savin & Adams, 1979) but significantly reduced (10%) when breathing 0.75 ppm ozone (Folinsbee et al., 1977). Exposure to 0.75 ppm ozone also reduces maximal work rate and maximal heart rate (Folinsbee et al., 1977). The reduction in $\dot{V}O_2$max is thought to be due to the reduction in $\dot{V}_E$max and may be a consequence of respiratory discomfort. Neither anaerobic threshold nor maximal work rate for 30 minutes of exercise were reduced by ozone concentrations of 0.3 ppm or less (Savin & Adams, 1979).

Peroxyacetyl Nitrate

Prolonged exercise during exposure to 0.24 ppm PAN appears to have little effect on cardiovascular or pulmonary function (Gliner et al., 1975; Raven, Gliner, & Sutton, 1976). The one exception is forced vital capacity (FVC), which was reduced 4% following a 4-hour exposure to PAN (Raven et al., 1976). The decrease in FVC is thought to be due to slight reductions in both inspiratory capacity and the expiratory reserve volume. Younger men appear to be more affected by exposure to PAN than older men. Shorter exercise and exposure periods to the same concentration of PAN have failed to produce any significant changes in pulmonary function (Raven et al., 1974). PAN may have a significant subjective effect on performance because it irritates the eyes. Subjects complain more frequently of irritation when exposed to PAN than during carbon monoxide or filtered air exposure (Gliner et al., 1975).

AIR POLLUTION MIXTURES

Air pollutants usually occur as mixtures of two or more pollutants. For example, photochemical smog usually contains ozone, nitrogen dioxide, and peroxyacetyl nitrate. The effects of breathing a mixture of pollutants may be different from those while breathing each pollutant separately. Two pollutants could react with one another to minimize or nullify the effects of one or both pollutants individually. It is also possible that the two pollutants could act in an additive fashion, with the effects being the sum of the effects of the two individual pollutants. Or the two pollutants may interact synergistically to produce a greater effect in the mixture than the sum of the individual pollutant effects.

Photochemical Oxidants

Several studies have examined the effects of exercise during periods of photochemical smog. Distance runners had slower running times on days with high levels of oxidant air pollution than on days with little air pollution (Wayne, Wehrle, & Carroll, 1967). Performance correlated highly ($r = 0.88$) with the oxidant level for the hour preceeding the race. Reductions in FVC, inspiratory capacity, and tidal volume have been found after a 2-hour football practice on days when the oxidant levels reached Stage 1 alert levels (McCafferty, Clamp, Straker, & Fee, 1979). Children exposed to high levels of pollution during exercise experienced a greater decrease in FEV_1 and FVC than children who exercised indoors (Lebowitz et all, 1974). Reductions in FVC and FEV_1 were also observed in a group of adolescents after a 20-mile hike.

Pollutant Combinations

One method of determining which pollutants are affecting the physiological responses is to study the pollutants individually and in combinations. Several combinations have been studied using this technique. The most widely studied combination has been carbon monoxide and PAN. Both are likely to be found in areas where the main pollutant is automobile exhaust and there is plenty of sunshine for photochemical oxidants to form. Low levels of CO (50 ppm) and PAN (0.24 ppm) appear to have little effect on aerobic capacity or cardiovascular responses to exercise either singly or combined (Gliner et al., 1975; Raven et al., 1974). However, during prolonged exercise the combination of PAN and CO reduced FVC 7% (Raven et al., 1976). The presence of PAN in the mixture also caused an increase in complaints about eye irritation (Gliner et al., 1975).

Another combination that has been studied with mixed results is ozone and sulfur dioxide. This mixture would be likely to occur where photochemical oxidants are formed and sulfur-containing fuels are burned. One study reported a synergistic effect of 0.37 ppm ozone + 0.37 ppm SO_2 on pulmonary function (Hazucha & Bates, 1975). The combination of pollutants produced a greater decrease in maximal midexpiratory flow than either pollutant alone. More recent work using approximately the same concentrations of both gases (0.4 ppm ozone and SO_2) also found decreases in pulmonary function, but the changes with the mixture were the same as those with ozone alone (Bedi, et al., 1979).

Sulfur dioxide and nitrogen dioxide may be found in combination where sulfur-containing fuels are burned. A mixture of 0.5 ppm SO_2 and 0.5 ppm NO_2 has no effect on pulmonary function measurements in normal adults (Linn et all, 1980). Slightly lower levels of SO_2 (0.3 ppm) also had little effect on the pulmonary function of asthmatics. However, subjective symptoms (cough, nasal discharge, wheezing) increased in both groups after exposure to the pollutant mixture.

Unfortunately, several combinations of pollutants (e.g., ozone and CO) that may coexist in the environment have not been studied. Because both ozone and CO have been found to affect performance by reducing $\dot{V}O_2max$, the effects of the combined pollutants during prolonged exercise should be investigated.

POLLUTANTS AND THE ENVIRONMENT

Hot Environments

So far we have examined the effects of various pollutants on physiological responses without considering other environmental factors that may influence the responses. Photochemical smog most frequently occurs during warm weather. Most studies are conducted in laboratories where the temperature is maintained between 21° and 25° C. However, several studies have examined the influence of increased ambient temperature on the responses to several of the pollutants. Increasing the ambient temperature to 35° C results in an increase in heart rate during exercise but does not alter the cardiovascular response to either carbon monoxide or PAN (Gliner et al., 1975). Maximal aerobic capacity is reduced more by heat than by 50 ppm CO, but exercise time is reduced more by 50 ppm CO than by filtered air in a warm environment (Drinkwater et al., 1974).

Warm environments appear to have a greater effect on the responses to ozone than to either CO or PAN. Vital capacity and MVV were reduced the most after exposure to 0.5 ppm ozone at 35° C (Folinsbee et al., 1977). Because ventilation during exercise was greater during heat exposure, more ozone would have entered the airways at 35° C than at lower temperatures. Because elevated ozone levels frequently coincide with ambient temperatures of 30° C and above, both are likely to be elevated during air pollution episodes.

Altitude

Increased levels of carbon monoxide are observed at moderate altitudes because of the incomplete combustion of fuel due to the lack of oxygen. Both altitude and CO cause hypoxia. The reduction in $\dot{V}O_2max$ with a 20% COHb is similar to the response to 4,000-m altitude (Vogel, Gleser, Wheeler, & Whitten, 1972). At 1,600 m, increasing COHb from 1% to 5% results in a 3.5% reduction in $\dot{V}O_2max$ and a 10% decrease in total work (Weiser, Morrill, Dickey, Kurt, & Cropp, 1978). The decline in aerobic capacity and work produced by CO is no greater at altitude than at sea level, which suggests that the two factors are additive rather than synergistic.

Carbon monoxide levels are also increased by smoking at altitude. Increasing the COHb to 4% at 3,050 m increases cardiac output and decreases the $a-\bar{v}O_2$ difference during moderate exercise in nonsmokers above responses that would occur with 4% COHb at sea level or with filtered air at altitude (Wagner, Horvath, Andrew, Cottle, & Bedi, 1978). Smokers appeared to be less affected by either altitude or 4% COHb levels.

TRAINING AND PERFORMANCE IN POLLUTED ENVIRONMENTS

Training

Should athletes train in polluted environments? For many athletes there is no choice. They live and work in metropolitan areas where air pollution is a fact of life. The question should be how to minimize the exposure to pollutants. This depends to some extent on the specific pollutant. Carbon monoxide levels are highest during the morning and evening rush hours. Ozone levels, on the other hand, begin to rise after sunrise, reach a peak during the early afternoon and fall after sunset (see Figure 5.4). Ozone levels also tend to be greatest during the summer and early fall, while CO and SO_2 levels are highest during the winter.

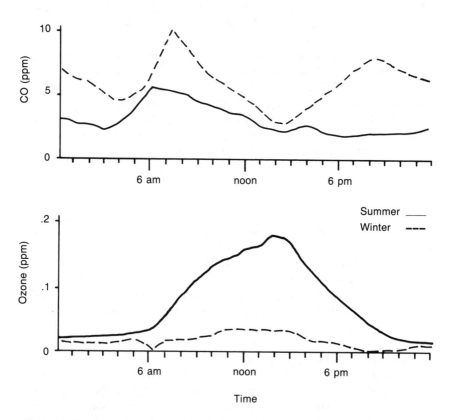

Figure 5.4. Ozone and carbon monoxide data in the Los Angeles area reflect both daily and seasonal fluctuations. Source: South Coast Air Quality Management District.

Note. From *Air pollution and athletic performance* (p. 45) by W.B. McCafferty, 1981, Springfield: Charles C. Thomas. Reprinted with permission.

To avoid elevated ozone concentrations, athletes should train early in the morning or in the evening during the summer (McCafferty, 1981). This will also allow the athlete to avoid training during the hottest part of the day. Because the effects of heat and ozone appear to be additive (Folinsbee, et al., 1977), athletes should avoid exercise during the afternoon, when both are near their peaks. Although people adapt to ozone after several days' exposure, deliberate exposure to ozone is not advised because of the possible harmful effects (McCafferty, 1981).

Runners and cyclists are most likely to be affected by elevated CO levels in the environment. CO levels are highest along heavily traveled streets and highways during the rush hour, and they reach a peak at stop signs and traffic lights when several cars are waiting with idling motors (Haagen-Smit, 1966). Joggers who run along busy streets during the rush hour increase their COHb level to 4% to 5% (Nicholson & Case, 1983). To minimize CO exposure, athletes should avoid training on heavily traveled roads and streets and train at times of the day when there is little traffic.

Athletes traveling to events are also exposed to CO while driving in rush hour traffic and when persons riding in the vehicle are smoking. Because it may take several hours for the CO to leave the blood, travel should be planned to avoid periods of heavy traffic. Smoking in indoor athletic facilities increases the CO concentration of the air. While the increase in CO may not affect the spectators, it is a potential problem for the athletes. McCafferty (1981) suggests that smoking be prohibited whenever athletes are present in automobiles and in all indoor athletic facilities, including swimming pools, locker rooms, arenas, and enclosed stadiums.

Performance

Few studies have examined the effects of air pollutants on exercise performance. Wayne et al. (1967) observed that runners have slower times on days with high air pollutant levels than when air pollution is low. Performance during the cross-country run correlated best with the oxidant air levels during the hour preceding the race. Ozone is the principal oxidant in photochemical smog. Maximal oxygen intake is reduced by elevated ozone levels (Folinsbee et al., 1977). If the runners' $\dot{V}O_2max$ were reduced, then the speed (intensity) of the run would also decrease. Other factors that may be involved in reducing performance in the presence of elevated ozone levels include irritation of the air passageways, which stimulates coughing, substernal pain, and a reduction in inspiratory capacity. The inability to breathe deeply may cause the runner to slow his or her pace.

The 1984 Olympic Games in Los Angeles took place in the summer months, when the ozone concentration is likely to be greatest. During July and August ozone levels exceed 0.2 ppm on 4 out of every 5 days and 0.35 ppm on 1 out of 5 days in the areas of Los Angeles where many of the events were held

(Korcok, 1981). These levels of ozone represent the Stage 1 Health Advisory and Stage 2 Warning emergency criteria, respectively, in California.

Should athletes compete when ozone levels increase to Stage 2 or Stage 3 (0.5 ppm ozone) air pollution episodes? No. Because of the higher ventilation rates, athletes inhale a greater quantity of ozone and are therefore more likely to be affected than spectators. Many athletic events have been canceled in the Los Angeles area during air pollution episodes. Just as heat stress during the middle of the day can present a serious health problem to the exercising person, elevated ozone levels also pose a health risk. During the months when ozone levels are greatest, it would be best to schedule athletic events (e.g., distance runs, swim meets) early in the morning or after sunset whenever possible.

There is little disagreement that carbon monoxide reduces aerobic performance when the COHb level exceeds approximately 4%. Carbon monoxide also appears to reduce arousal. The ability to detect a signal decreases when the COHb level exceeds 5% (Gliner, Horvath, & Mihevic, 1983). Reduced aerobic capacity would affect all sports that require cardiovascular endurance, including distance running, cycling, swimming, field hockey, and soccer. Reduced signal detection has implications for all sports that require the participant to track a ball and also be aware of the position of opponents and teammates. These sports include most of the team sports, such as football, basketball, and ice hockey.

Fortunately, most sports that are likely to be affected by elevated CO levels are performed outdoors. The two sports with the greatest risk of CO exposure are running and cycling. Most road races are scheduled on weekends, which avoids heavy traffic. To further minimize exposure to CO, all motor vehicles, including police and press vehicles, should be banned from the race course during the race. Carbon monoxide levels in indoor arenas and swimming pools can be reduced by banning smoking inside the buildings. If the ambient CO level reaches the emergency action level (40 ppm over an 8-hour period), sporting events should be canceled or postponed.

SUMMARY

Air pollutants affect the body in several ways. Carbon monoxide binds to hemoglobin and reduces the amount of oxygen in the blood. Ozone and sulfur dioxide irritate the respiratory passageways, while PAN irritates the eyes. The presence of particulate matter may facilitate the passage of sulfur dioxide into the smaller airways.

More air moves in and out of the lungs during exercise, which brings more pollutants in contact with the mucous membranes than during resting conditions. Because the exercising individual is likely to breathe through the mouth, the scrubbing action of the nasal mucosa, which removes several of the pollutants, is bypassed. The result is a lower threshold concentration for ozone and sulfur dioxide during exercise than at rest. Carbon monoxide decreases maximal aerobic capacity when the COHb level is above 4%.

Because athletes are more likely to be affected by air pollutants than sedentary individuals, athletes should avoid exposure to pollutants before and during exercise. In areas where ozone is the major pollutant, exposure can be minimized by training early in the day or after dark. Exposure to carbon monoxide can be reduced by avoiding heavily traveled streets and highways during the rush hours. During air pollution episodes when pollutants reach emergency action levels, training and competition should be postponed or canceled.

6

The Traveling Athlete

Travel may present problems for the amateur, professional, and recreational athlete, especially if there is a change in environmental conditions. Some of the common problems traveling athletes encounter will be discussed in this chapter. Questions that will be discussed include:

- Is there a way of reducing the effects of altitude on performance?
- What special precautions are needed before exercising in cold environments?
- How can a person prepare ahead for exercise in hot environments?
- Is there a way to prepare for air pollution?
- What happens to body rhythms when a person crosses several time zones?
- Does jet lag affect performance?
- What strategies will reduce jet lag?

THE PROBLEM

Many athletes must travel across the continent or to other continents to compete. Professional baseball and football teams, for example, are located on both the east and west coasts of the United States. These athletes fly across the North American continent several times during a season. Top amateur athletes in track and field, skiing, and ice and speed skating compete on a regular basis in Europe as well as in North America and may travel to Asia and Australia for competition.

Such travel may result in a change in the environment that the athlete is used to competing in. Travel across the equator means a change in the season.

Athletes training during the middle of the winter in North America may suddenly find themselves competing in the middle of the summer in Australia or South America. Collegiate athletes who usually train near sea level may find themselves competing at moderate altitude against athletes from the Universities of Colorado and Wyoming or the Air Force Academy.

In some of these cases, the change in environment could adversely affect performance. For example, a skier from New England might experience acute mountain sickness while competing in the Rocky Mountains, or a distance runner from Finland could experience heat exhaustion while competing in Los Angeles. Such drastic changes in the environment require planning on the part of the coaches and athletes for best results.

Recreational sports enthusiasts may also experience a drastic change in the environment in pursuing their favorite sport. Many lowlanders fly to ski resorts in the Rocky Mountains and Sierras for a week of skiing each winter. Trekkers fly to high-altitude airports in Nepal for a quick climb in the Himalayas. Tennis and golf enthusiasts from the northern United States and Canada schedule mid-winter and spring vacations in the Sunbelt to get in a little early practice and competition. These recreational athletes can also suffer adverse effects from a change in environment and they should also plan ahead. This chapter presents practical guidelines for traveling athletes.

PLANNING AHEAD

Altitude

Most problems encountered by athletes changing altitudes can be minimized or eliminated with planning. Lowlanders who know they will compete at altitude during the season should plan their arrival at altitude either right before the event if it is a 1-day event or several weeks in advance if the competition will take place over several days or weeks. Unfortunately, not all athletes will have the luxury of spending several weeks acclimatizing to altitude before competition because of their jobs and school work. For example, most collegiate skiers cannot afford the time to spend several weeks acclimatizing to altitude when the National Collegiate Athletic Association Championships are scheduled for a site in the Rocky Mountains. Neither can the recreational skier who has a 1-week vacation afford the time necessary for acclimatization.

The following suggestions are made for those persons who must travel rapidly to altitude with little time for acclimatization:

1. If possible, plan to arrive 2 to 3 days before competition. Acute mountain sickness usually occurs within the first 24 hours at altitude and subsides after 72 hours.
2. Reduce physical activity during the first day at altitude.

3. Consume a high-carbohydrate diet for a couple of days before and after arriving at altitude.
4. If you are flying into moderately high altitudes, take acetazolamide the day before and after arrival.
5. Consume large quantities of fluids while at altitude to prevent dehydration.
6. If you are climbing, limit the vertical gain to 300 m per day. At higher altitudes it is a good idea to spend several days at one altitude before resuming your climb. This will allow for some acclimatization.
7. Evacuate persons exhibiting symptoms of high-altitude pulmonary edema or cerebral edema to a lower altitude immediately.
8. High altitudes also mean colder temperatures. Go prepared for this. Mountain climbers and backcountry travelers should have adequate clothing for temperatures below freezing and be prepared for blizzard conditions even during the summer.

Cold

Cold environmental conditions are most often encountered during the winter months and can easily be planned for by the traditional winter sports athlete and enthusiast. One of the simplest ways to prepare for outdoor activity is to dress in layers. If the temperature is low when you first begin exercising, you will need several layers of clothing to keep warm. As your body temperature increases, you should discard the outer garments before you begin to sweat! Excess sweat in clothing can be chilling—even deadly—in winter, so pay particular attention to ventilating your body when you are active in the cold. If the ambient temperature rises during the activity, you may have to remove more layers. Take special precautions to protect exposed areas when the wind chill index is low to prevent frostbite.

Most cases of hypothermia occur in mountain climbers, cross-country skiers, and backcountry travelers who get caught in blizzards or bad weather. Inadequate clothing is one of the most important factors predisposing a person to hypothermia. Backcountry travelers (climbers, hikers, and skiers) should wear or carry a water-impermeable outer garment to prevent inner clothing layers from becoming wet. Most materials are poor insulators when wet. Avoid alcoholic beverages while in the cold, because heat is lost at a faster rate and blood glucose levels drop after drinking alcohol.

Performance in both endurance and power events is likely to be adversely affected by the cold if body temperatures decrease. It is important to keep warm by performing physical activity or by adding extra layers of clothing when sedentary. Performance in sports with intermittent activity is more likely to be affected than in sports with continuous activity. Professional football teams must sometimes play in blizzard conditions in the northern United States during December. Adequate clothing must be provided on the sidelines to prevent muscles from cooling. Fortunately many spring sporting events (e.g., baseball games, tennis matches) are postponed by rain. It is much more difficult to keep the body warm when clothing is wet. If you are participating in an activity that may continue in cold, rainy weather (e.g., hiking, golf tournaments), it is a good idea to carry water-repellent clothing with you.

Hot Environments

Athletes and sports enthusiasts who will be traveling to an area where the ambient temperature is above 25.6° C (80° F) should become heat acclimatized before participating in an event in the warm climate, unless the ambient temperature is the same or higher in the environment where you are training and competing, in which case, you will already be acclimatized to the heat. Athletes who will need to acquire some heat acclimatization should plan to arrive at the site 1 week before the competition. This early arrival will allow you to train in the heat and gain sufficient acclimatization. During the first 2 or 3 days of acclimatization, you will probably need to reduce the intensity and/or duration of training. If an early arrival in the hot environment is not possible, you can acclimatize to some extent by wearing added layers of clothing while training.

Sudden heat waves may affect most of the athletes participating in an event. Because it is unlikely that there will be any advance warning, there will be little opportunity for athletes to become acclimatized. In this instance the athlete should pay special attention to fluid intake before, during, and after training and competition. Lack of adequate fluid replacement predisposes a person to heat illness. Athletes who have flown to the site of competition are likely to be dehydrated because of the low humidity in the airplane cabin (Ehret & Scanlon, 1983). To prevent dehydration during the flight, the traveler should drink lots of fluids. The consumption of alcoholic beverages should be limited or avoided, because alcohol increases the amount of fluid lost in the urine. Body fluid losses have not been replenished when thirst is satisfied. To make sure that fluid losses have been replaced, athletes should weigh themselves at the same time every day. A decrease in body weight means body fluids have not been replaced.

Special attention to clothing is also beneficial in a hot environment. Loose, light-weight clothing facilitates air movement near the skin and the evaporation of sweat. When solar radiation is high, clothing color is also an important factor. White and light-colored clothing reflects more heat than dark colors. Wearing a hat is also beneficial, because it reduces the amount of heat gained through the head. In hot, humid environments less of the skin surface should be covered with clothing. Fabrics that wick moisture away from the skin (e.g., cotton) are preferred in hot environments.

Air Pollution

There appears to be little that the athlete should do before performing in an area where considerable air pollution may be experienced. Although some adaptation may occur with repeated exposures to carbon monoxide and ozone, the disadvantages are likely to outweigh the advantages. Because both carbon monoxide and ozone reduce $\dot{V}O_2max$, training will probably be hindered when one or both pollutants are present in the environment. If an air pollution episode should occur at the time of a scheduled competition, athletes should minimize their exposure to the pollutants by remaining indoors as much as possible.

TRANSMERIDIAN TRAVEL

The traveling athlete may cross several time zones to reach the site of competition. For example, professional baseball teams located on the West Coast will travel across three time zones to play in New York, while professional golfers playing in the British Open will experience a 5-hour time difference between the East Coast of the United States and Scotland. Travel across time zones leads to a disruption in the normal daily rhythm of body functions. These daily rhythms, known as circadian rhythms, have been observed for body temperature, heart rate, hormone secretion, and excretion of electrolytes. An example of the circadian rhythm for rectal temperature is shown in Figure 6.1.

Circadian rhythms are internal rhythms that are set or entrained by different cues called zeitgebers (time givers). One important zeitgeber is the presence or absence of light. Other zeitgebers include meal times, physical activity, clocks, and sleep time (Klein & Wegmann, 1980). Rapid travel across several time zones leads to desynchronization of circadian rhythms, commonly known as jet lag.

Jet Lag

When a person travels from the East Coast to the West Coast of the United States, 3 hours will be added to the normal day. Westward flights lead to phase delays in the normal circadian rhythm (Figure 6.2a). Over a period of several days the circadian rhythm for core temperature will shift to that of the new time zone. Each day core temperature will reach its highest and lowest points approximately 1 hour later until it adjusts to the normal rhythm of the new time zone. On the other hand, after an eastward flight a traveler will adapt to the new time zone by phase advances (Figure 6.2b). In this case, core temperature will reach its highest and lowest points 1 hour earlier each day.

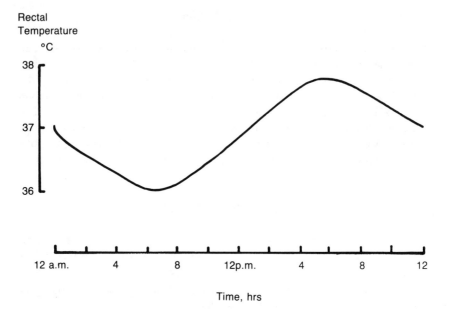

Figure 6.1. Circadian rhythm for rectal temperature.

There is some evidence that adjustment to a new time zone is more rapid after westward flights than after eastward flights. Klein and Wegmann (1980) reported that travelers resynchronized their circadian rhythms at the rate of 90 min per day after westward flights and 60 min per day after eastward flights.

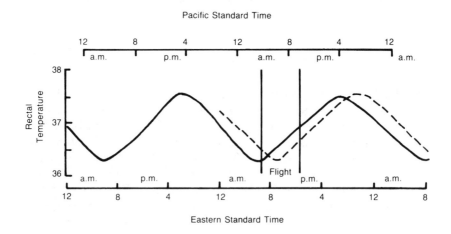

Figure 6.2a. Westward flight illustrating phase delay between the old—and new—rhythms.

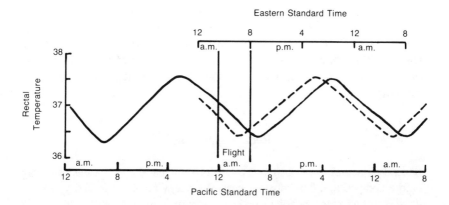

Figure 6.2b. Eastward flight illustrating phase advance between old—and new—rhythm.

In other words, it should take approximately 3 days to adjust to the Eastern time zone after a flight from Los Angeles, but only 2 days to adapt to the Pacific time zone after a flight from Boston.

For the athlete traveling to a new time zone, the change in circadian rhythm may have a detrimental effect on performance. If a baseball player flies from Atlanta to San Diego on the morning of an 8 p.m. Pacific Daylight Time (PDT) game, it will be 11 p.m. Eastern Daylight Time (EDT) when the game starts and about 2 a.m. EDT when the game ends. Performance in the evening is most likely to be affected on the first day after westward flights (Klein & Wegmann, 1980). The golfer who flies from Toronto to Glasgow, a difference of 5 hours, and then has an 8 a.m. tee time will actually be teeing off at 3 a.m. (EDT). After eastward flights performance in the morning is likely to be affected for the first few days.

Frequently mentioned symptoms of jet lag are tiredness, insomnia, and weakness (Wright, Vogel, Sampson, Knapik, Patton, & Daniels, 1983). Other symptoms include gastrointestinal disturbances, headache, loss of appetite, and impaired peripheral vision (Ehret & Scanlon, 1983). There is some evidence that cognitive abilities may be impaired immediately after a time zone shift. During the first day after a 6-hour time zone shift, Graeber (1980) found 10% to 15% decrements in several cognitive tests. Test scores returned to the preflight level after 3 days in the new time zone.

Physical performance also appears to be affected by jet lag. Both dynamic strength and muscular endurance decrease immediately after a 6-hour shift in the time zones (Wright et al., 1983). Performance times for a sprint and a middle-distance run increased for several days after the flight. However, there was no decrement in maximal aerobic capacity after the time zone shift. Performance in team sports such as volleyball and ice hockey may also be affected for several days after a change in time zones (Sasaki, 1980). Sleep deprivation may be implicated in performance reduction after transmeridian flights. Several studies have shown a reduction in endurance when subjects have been deprived of sleep for 36 hours or longer (Martin, 1981; Martin & Chen, 1984), while other studies have found a slowing of reaction time and movement after sleep deprivation (Copes & Rosentswieg, 1972; Pickett & Morris, 1975).

Reducing Jet Lag

Several strategies have been suggested for reducing the symptoms of jet lag before competition. The most successful strategy has been to arrive several days early, allowing one day for each hour of time zone shift. This would mean, for example, that skiers flying from Denver to Zurich should arrive 8 days before a World Cup race to allow for the 8-hour shift in time zones. While this may be the best strategy, it may not always be practical. For example, the recreational skier flying to the Alps for a week's vacation would spend the entire week adapting to the new time zone. Another strategy that has been somewhat successful has been to stay in a neighboring time zone for several days before going to the site of competition (Sasaki, 1980). Several stopovers en route may reduce the symptoms, but it will take the same number of days to adjust to the new time zone.

The newest strategy involves the use of multiple zeitgebers to reset the circadian rhythm to the new time zone (Ehret, Groh, & Meinert, 1980; Ehret & Scanlon, 1983). Included among the multiple zeitgebers are

1. alternating days of fasting and feasting,
2. shifting meal times to that of the new time zone on the day of the flight,
3. use of the methyl xanthines in coffee, tea, colas, and chocolate to help in the phase shifts, and
4. consumption of high-protein and high-carbohydrate meals.

Fasting is included because fasting subjects adapt more readily to food given at a different time of day than subjects who have eaten (Ehret et al., 1980). The methyl xanthines (caffeine, theophylline, and theobromine) will produce phase delays when taken in the morning and phase advances if taken in the early evening. Because travelers heading west will experience a phase delay, they should drink beverages containing methyl xanthines in the morning. Persons heading east should not consume methyl xanthines until the early evening to help produce a phase advance. Meals high in protein are consumed at breakfast and lunch to stimulate the production of catecholamines and activity during the day (Ehret & Scanlon, 1983). High carbohydrate meals are eaten at supper to stimulate the production of the neurotransmitter serotonin and sleep. Studies with animals have shown that a high-protein breakfast stimulates a rapid

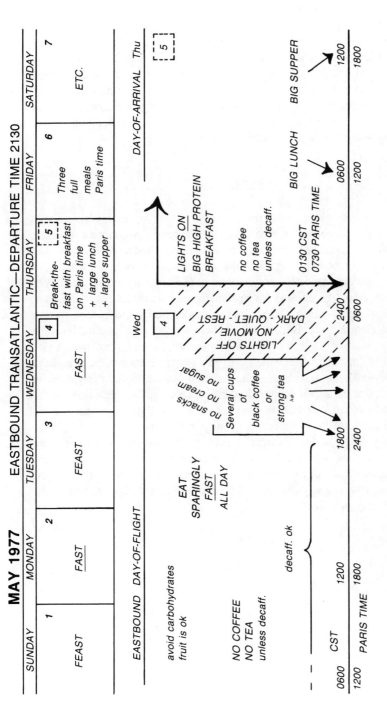

Figure 6.3 A diet plan for eastbound transatlantic travel.

Note. From "Circadian dyschronism and chronotypic ecophilia as factors in aging and longevity" (p. 198) by C.F. Ehret, K.R. Groh, and J.C. Meinert, 1978. In *Advances in experimental medicine and biology,* **108.** *Aging and biological rhythms.* Reprinted with permission.

adjustment to a new time zone, while low-protein breakfasts may delay the
adjustment for up to 1 week (Ehret et al., 1980).

Research has shown that the use of multiple zeitgebers by humans during
transmeridian flights is beneficial. Subjects who used multiple zeitgebers during transatlantic flights had less fatigue for several days after the flight compared with control subjects (Graeber, 1980). Figure 6.3 outlines some of the
procedures recommended by Ehret and Scanlon (1983) for reducing the effects of jet lag. For more detailed information on the use of multiple zeitgebers,
see *Overcoming Jet Lag* by Ehret and Scanlon.

SUMMARY

Today's athlete frequently finds travel necessary to compete. Such travel may
result in a drastic change in environments. Persons traveling to altitude for
competition or recreation will find that endurance is reduced. Because rapid
ascent increases the risk of altitude illness, planning is necessary when competition or recreational activities will occur at moderate or high altitudes. Adequate time should be allowed for acclimatization if competition will extend
over several days or weeks. Exposure to altitude usually also means exposure
to a cold environment. Backcountry travelers should carry extra layers of
clothing, including water-repellent outer garments, even during the summer.

Travel to hot environments poses a risk of heat illness for the unacclimatized individual. Because heat acclimatization occurs in just a few days, an
early arrival at the site of competition is advisable. Airline passengers should
be aware of the dehydration that occurs during the flights, and they should
consume adequate fluids before exercising in the heat.

Flights across time zones disrupt a person's normal circadian rhythm and
produce symptoms of jet lag. Jet lag may impair sports performance for several
days. It takes about 1 day for each hour difference in time zones for the various
circadian rhythms to resynchronize. Use of multiple zeitgebers before and after
the flight may help reduce jet lag.

Appendix A

Caloric Values for Oxygen Consumption

Nonprotein RQ	Kcal Per Liter Oxygen Consumed
0.707	4.686
.71	4.690
.72	4.702
.73	4.714
.74	4.727
.75	4.739
.76	4.751
.77	4.764
.78	4.776
.79	4.788
.80	4.801
.81	4.813
.82	4.825
.83	4.838
.84	4.850
.85	4.862
.86	4.875
.87	4.887
.88	4.899
.89	4.911
.90	4.924
.91	4.936
.92	4.948
.93	4.961
.94	4.973
.95	4.984
.96	4.998
.97	5.010
.98	5.022
.99	5.035
1.00	5.047

Adpated from McArdle, W.D., Katch, F.I., & Katch, V.L. *Exercise Physiology: Energy, Nutrition, and Human Performance*, Philadelphia: Lea & Febiger, 1981, p. 101.

Appendix B

AMERICAN COLLEGE OF SPORTS MEDICINE
Position Stand on
THE PREVENTION OF THERMAL INJURIES DURING DISTANCE RUNNING

Purpose of the Position Stand

1. To alert sponsors of distance-running events to potentially serious health hazards during distance running—especially thermal injury.
2. To advise sponsors to consult local weather history and plan events at times when the environmental heat stress would most likely be acceptable.
3. To encourage sponsors to identify the environmental heat stress existing on the day of a race and communicate this to the participants.
4. To educate participants regarding thermal injury susceptibility and prevention.
5. To inform sponsors of preventive actions which may reduce the frequency and severity of this type of injury.

This position stand replaces that of *"Prevention of Heat Injury During Distance Running,"* published by the American College of Sports Medicine in 1975. It has been expanded to consider thermal problems which may affect the general community of joggers, fun runners, and elite athletes who participate in distance-running events. Although hyperthermia is still the most common serious problem encountered in North American fun runs and races, hypothermia can be a problem for slow runners in long races such as the marathon, in cold and/or wet environmental conditions or following races when blood glucose is low and the body's temperature regulatory mechanism is impaired.

Because the physiological responses to exercise and environmental stress vary among participants, strict compliance with the recommendations, while helpful, will not guarantee complete protection from thermal illness. The general guidelines in this position stand do not constitute definitive medical advice, which should be sought from a physician for specific cases. Nevertheless, adherence to these recommendations should help to minimize the incidence of thermal injury.

POSITION STAND

1. **Medical Director**

    A medical director knowledgeable in exercise physiology and sports medicine should coordinate the preventive and therapeutic aspects of the running event and work closely with the race director.

2. **Race Organization**
    a) Races should be organized to avoid the hottest summer months and the hottest part of the day. As there are great regional variations in environmental conditions, the local weather history will be most helpful in scheduling an event to avoid times when an unacceptable level of heat stress is likely to prevail. Organizers should be cautious of unseasonably hot days in the early spring, as entrants will almost certainly not be heat acclimatized.
    b) The environmental heat stress prediction for the day should be obtained from the meteorological service. It can be measured as wet bulb globe temperature (WBGT) (see Appendix I), which is a temperature/humidity/radiation index (1). If WBGT is above 28° C (82° F), consideration should be given to rescheduling or delaying the race until safer conditions prevail. If below 28° C, participants may be alerted to the degree of heat stress by using color-coded flags at the start of the race and at key positions along the course (Appendix II; 26).
    c) All summer events should be scheduled for the early morning, ideally before 8:00 a.m., or in the evening after 6:00 p.m., to minimize solar radiation.
    d) An adequate supply of water should be available before the race and every 2-3 km during the race. Runners should be encouraged to consume 100-200 ml at each station.
    e) Race officials should be educated as to the warning signs of an impending collapse. Each official should wear an identifiable arm band

or bandage and should warn runners to stop if they appear to be in difficulty.

f) Adequate traffic and crowd control must be maintained at all times.

g) There should be a ready source of radio communications from various points on the course to a central organizing point to coordinate responses to emergencies.

3. a) **Medical Organization and Responsibility:**

The Medical Director should alert local hospitals and ambulance services to the event and should make prior arrangements with medical personnel for the care of casualties, especially those suffering from heat injury. The mere fact that an entrant signs a waiver in no way absolves the organizers of moral and/or legal responsibility. Medical personnel supervising races should have the authority to evaluate, examine, and/or stop a runner who displays the symptoms and signs of impending heat injury, or who appears to be mentally and/or physically out of control for any other reason.

b) **Medical Facilities:**

i. Medical support staff and facilities should be available at the race site.

ii. The facilities should be staffed with personnel capable of instituting immediate and appropriate resuscitation measures. Apart from the routine resuscitation equipment, ice packs and fans for cooling are required.

iii. Persons trained in first aid, appropriately identified with an arm band, badge, etc., should be stationed along the course to warn runners to stop if they exhibit signs of impending heat injury.

iv. Ambulances or vans with accompanying medical personnel should be available along the course.

v. Although the emphasis in this stand has been on the management of hyperthermia, on cold, wet, and windy days, athletes may be chilled and require "space blankets," blankets, and warm drinks at the finish to prevent or treat hypothermia (23, 45).

4. **Competitor Education**

The education of fun runners has increased greatly in recent years, but race organizers must not assume that all participants are well informed or prepared. Distributing guidelines at the pre-registration, publicity in the press, and holding clinics/seminars before runs are valuable.

The following persons are particularly prone to heat illness: the obese (3, 17, 43), unfit (13, 29, 39, 43), dehydrated (6, 14, 31, 37, 38, 47), those unacclimatized to the heat (20, 43), those with a previous history of heat stroke (36, 43), and anyone who runs while ill (41.). Children perspire less than adults and have a lower heat tolerance (2). Based on the above information, all participants should be advised of the following.

a) Adequate training and fitness are important for full enjoyment of the run and also to prevent heat-related injuries (13, 28, 29, 39).

b) Prior training in the heat will promote heat acclimatization and thereby reduce the risk of heat injury. It is wise to do as much training as possible at the time of day at which the race will be held (20).

c) Fluid consumption before and during the race will reduce the risk of heat injury, particularly in longer runs such as the marathon (6, 14, 47).

d) Illness prior to or at the time of the event should preclude competition (41).

e) Participants should be advised of the early symptoms of heat injury. These include clumsiness, stumbling, excessive sweating (and also cessation of sweating), headache, nausea, dizziness, apathy, and any gradual impairment of consciousness (42).

f) Participants should be advised to choose a comfortable speed and not to run faster than conditions warrant (18, 33).

g) Participants are advised to run with a partner, each being responsible for the other's well-being (33).

BACKGROUND FOR POSITION STAND

There has been an exponential rise in the number of fun runs and races in recent years and, as would be expected, a similar increase in the number of running-related injuries. Minor injuries such as bruises, blisters and musculoskeletal injuries are most common (41, 45). Myocardial infarction or cardiac arrest is, fortunately, very rare and occurs almost exclusively in patients with symptomatic heart disease (44). Hypoglycemia may be seen occasionally in normal runners (11) and has been observed following marathons (21) and shorter fun runs (41).

The most serious injuries in fun runs and races are related to problems of thermoregulation. In the shorter races, 10 km (6.2 miles) or less, hyperthermia with the attendant problems of heat exhaustion and heat syncope dominates, even on relatively cool days (4, 5, 10, 15, 16, 18, 27, 41). In longer races, heat problems are common on warm or hot days (31), but on moderate to cold days, hypothermia may be a real risk to some participants (23).

Thermoregulation and hyperthermia. Fun runners may experience hyperthermia or hypothermia, depending on the environmental conditions and clothing worn. The adequately clothed runner is capable of withstanding a wide range of environmental temperatures. Hyperthermia is the potential problem in warm and hot weather, when the body's rate of heat production is greater than its ability to dissipate this heat (1). In cold weather, scanty clothing may provide inadequate protection from the environment and hypothermia may develop, particularly towards the end of a long race when running speed and, therefore, heat production, are reduced.

During intense exercise, heat production in contracting muscles is 15-20 times that of basal metabolism and is sufficient to raise body core temperature in an average size individual by 1° C every 5 min if no temperature-regulating mechanisms were activated (25). With increased heat production, thermal receptors in the hypothalamus sense the increased body temperature and respond with an increased cutaneous circulation; thus, the excess heat is transferred to the skin surface to be dissipated by physical means, primarily the evaporation of sweat (9). The precise quantitative relationships in heat transfer are beyond the scope of this position stand, but are well reviewed elsewhere (24, 25).

When the rate of heat production exceeds that of heat loss for a sufficient period of time, thermal injury will occur. In long races, sweat loss can be significant and result in a total body water deficit of 6-10% of body weight (47). Such dehydration will subsequently reduce sweating and predispose the runner to hyperthermia, heat stroke, heat exhaustion, and muscle cramps (47). For a given level of dehydration, children have a greater increase in core temperature than do adults (2). Rectal temperatures have been reported above 40.6° C after races and fun runs (7, 22, 31, 35) and as high as 42-43° C in fun run participants who have collapsed (32, 34, 41, 42).

Fluid ingestion before and during prolonged running will minimize dehydration (and reduce the rate of increase in body core temperature) (7, 14). However, in fun runs of less than 10 km, hyperthermia may occur in the absence of significant dehydration (41). Runners should avoid consuming large quantities of highly concentrated sugar solution during runs, as this may result in a decrease in gastric emptying (8, 12).

Thermoregulation and hypothermia. Heat can be lost readily from the body when the rate of heat production is exceeded by heat loss (46). Even on moderately cool days, if the pace slows and/or if weather conditions become cooler en route, hypothermia may ensue (23). Several deaths have been reported from hypothermia during fun runs in mountain environments (30, 40). Hypothermia is common in inexperienced marathon runners who frequently run the second half of the race much more slowly than the first half. Such runners may be able to maintain core temperature initially, but with the slow pace of the second half, especially on cool, wet, or windy days, hypothermia can develop (23).

Early symptoms and signs of hypothermia include shivering, euphoria, and an appearance of intoxication. As core temperature continues to fall, shivering may stop, lethargy and muscular weakness may occur with disorientation, hallucinations, and often a combative nature. If core temperature falls below 30° C, the victim may lose consciousness.

Organizers of distance races and fun runs and their medical support staff should anticipate the medical problems and be capable of responding to significant numbers of hyperthermic and/or hypothermic runners. Thermal injury can be minimized with appropriate education of participants and with adequate facilities, supplies, and support staff.

Appendix I
Measurement of Environmental Heat Stress

Ambient temperature is only one component of environmental heat stress; others are humidity, wind velocity, and radiant heat. Therefore, measurement of ambient temperature, dry bulb alone, is inadequate. The most useful and widely applied approach is wet bulb globe temperature (WBGT).

$$WBGT = (0.7\ Twb) + (0.2\ Tg) + (0.1\ Tdb),$$

where Twb = temperature (wet bulb thermometer), Tg = temperature (black globe thermometer), and Tdb = temperature (dry bulb thermometer).

The importance of wet bulb temperature can be readily appreciated, as it accounts for 70% of the index, whereas dry bulb temperature accounts for only 10%. A simple portable heat stress monitor which gives direct WBGT in degrees C or degrees F to monitor conditions during fun runs has proven useful (19).

Alternatively, if a means for readily assessing WBGT is not available from wet bulb, globe, and dry bulb temperatures, one can use the following equation (48).

$$WBGT = (0.567\ Tdb) + (0.393\ Pa) + 3.94,$$

where Tdb = temperature (dry bulb thermometer) and Pa = environmental water vapor pressure. These environmental variables should be readily available from local weather or radio stations.

Instruments to measure WBGT are available commercially. Additional information may be obtained from the American College of Sports Medicine.

Appendix II
Use of Color-Coded Flags to Indicate the Risk of
Thermal Stress*

1. A RED FLAG: High Risk: When WBGT is 23-28° C (73-82° F). This signal would indicate that all runners should be aware that heat injury is possible and any person particularly sensitive to heat or humidity should probably not run.

2. AN AMBER FLAG: Moderate Risk: When WBGT is 18-23° C (65-73° F).
   It should be remembered that the air temperature, probably humidity, and almost certainly the radiant heat at the beginning of the race will increase during the course of the race if conducted in the morning or early afternoon.
3. A GREEN FLAG: Low Risk: When WBGT is below 18° C (65° F).
   This in no way guarantees that heat injury will not occur, but indicates only that the risk is low.
4. A WHITE FLAG: Low Risk for hyperthermia, but possible risk of hypothermia: When WBGT is below 10° C (50° F).
   Hypothermia may occur, especially in slow runners in long races, and in wet and windy conditions.
* This scale is determined for runners clad in running shorts, shoes and a T-shirt. In warmer weather, the less clothing the better. For males, wearing no shirt or a mesh top is better than wearing a T-shirt because the surface for evaporation is increased. However, in areas where radiant heat is excessive, a light top may be helpful.

Appendix III
Road Race Checklist

Medical Personnel

1. Have aid personnel available if the race is 10 km (6.2 miles) or longer, and run in warm or cold weather.
2. Recruit back-up personnel from existing emergency medical services (police, fire rescue, emergency medical service).
3. Notify local hospitals of the time and place of the road race.

Aid Stations

1. Provide major aid station at the finish point which is cordoned off from public access.
2. Equip the major aid station with the following supplies:
   — tent
   — cots
   — bath towels
   — water in large containers
   — ice in bag or ice chest or quick-cold packs
   — hose with spray nozzle
   — tables for medical supplies and equipment
   — stethoscopes
   — blood pressure cuffs
   — rectal thermometers or meters (range up to 43° C)
   — dressings

— blankets
— aluminum thermal sheets (''space blankets'')
— elastic bandages
— splints
— skin disinfectants
— intravenous fluids (supervision by a physician is required).

3. Position aid stations along the route at 4 km (2.5 mile) intervals for races over 10 km and at the halfway point for shorter races.
4. Stock each aid station with enough fluid (cool water is the optimum) for each runner to have 300-360 ml (10-12 ounces) at each aid station. A margin of 25% additional cups should be available to account for spillage and double usage.

Communications/Surveillance
1. Set up communication between the medical personnel and the major aid station.
2. Arrange for a radio-equipped car or van to follow the race course, and provide radio contact with director.

Instruction to Runners
1. Appraise the race participants of potential medical problems in advance of the race so precautions may be followed.
2. Advise the race director to announce the following information by loudspeaker immediately prior to the race:
   — the flag color; the risks for hyperthermia and/or hypothermia
   — location of aid stations and type of fluid available
   — reinforcement of warm weather or cold weather self-care.
3. Advise the race participants to print their names, addresses, and any medical problems on the back of the registration number.

Appendix IV
Medical Stations
General Guidelines

Staff for Large Races
1. Physician, podiatrist, nurse or EMT, a team of 3 per 1,000 runners. Double or triple this number at the finish area.
2. One ambulance per 3,000 runners at finish area; one cruising vehicle.
3. One physician to act as triage officer at finish.

Water
Estimate 1 liter (0.26 gallon) per runner per 16 km (10 miles), or roughly, per 60-90 min running time, and depending on number of stations.
For 10 km, the above rule is still recommended.

Table 1. Equipment needed at aid stations and the field hospital (per 1,000 runners).

Aid Stations

No.	Item
	ice in small plastic bags or quick-cold packs
5	stretchers (10 at 10 km and beyond)
5	blankets (10 at 10 km and beyond)
6 each	6 inch and 4 inch elastic bandages
½ case	4 × 4 inch gauze pads
½ case	surgical soap
	small instrument kits
	adhesive strips
	moleskin
½ case	petroleum jelly
2 each	inflatable arm and leg splints
	athletic trainer's kit

Field Hospital

No.	Item
10	stretchers
4	sawhorses
10-20	blankets (depending on environmental conditions)
10	intravenous set-ups
2 each	inflatable arm and leg splints
2 cases	1½ inch tape
2 cases each	elastic bandages (2, 4, and 6 inches)
2 cases	sheet wadding
	underwrap
2 cases	4 × 4 inch gauze pads
	adhesive strips
	moleskin
½ case	surgical soap
2	oxygen tanks with regulators and masks
2	ECG monitors with defibrillators
	ice in small plastic bags
	small instrument kits

Adapted from reference 26.

Cups = (number of entrants × number of stations) + 25% additional per
station.
     = (2 × number or entrants) extra at finish area.

Double this total if the course is out and back.
In cold weather, an equivalent amount of warm drinks should be available.

References

1. ADOLPH, E.I., *Physiology of Man in the Desert*. New York: Interscience, 1947, pp. 5-43.
2. BAR-OR, O. Climate and the exercising child—a review. *Int. J. Sports Med.* 1:53-65, 1980.
3. BAR-OR, O., H.M. LUNDEGREN, and E.R. BUSKIRK. Heat tolerance of exercising lean and obese women. *J. Appl. Physiol.* 26:403-409, 1969.
4. BUSKIRK, E.R., P.F. IAMPIETRO, and D.E. BASS. Work performance after dehydration: effects of physical conditioning and heat acclimatization. *J. Appl. Physiol.* 12:189-194, 1958.
5. CLOWES, G.H.A., JR. and T.F. O'DONNELL, JR. Heat stroke. *N. Engl. J. Med.* 291:564-567, 1974.
6. COSTILL, D.L., R. COTE, E. MILLER, T. MILLER, AND S. WYNDER. Water and electrolyte replacement during days of work in the heat. *Avait. Space Environ. Med.* 46:795-800, 1970.
7. COSTILL, D.L., W.F. KAMMER, and A. FISHER. Fluid ingestion during distance running. *Arch. Environ. Health* 21:520-525, 1970.
8. COSTILL, D.L., and B. SALTIN. Factors limiting gastric emptying during rest and exercise. *J. Appl. Physiol.* 37:679-683, 1974.
9. ELLIS, F.P., A.N. EXTON-SMITH, K.G. FOSTER, and J.S. WEINER. Eccrine sweating and mortality during heat waves in very young and very old persons. *Isr. J. Med. Sci.* 12:815-817, 1976.
10. ENGLAND, A.C., III, D.W. FRASER, A.W. HIGHTOWER, et al. Preventing severe heat injury in runners: suggestions from the 1979 Peachtree Roach Race experience. *Ann. Intern. Med.* 97: 196-201, 1982.
11. FELIG, P., A. CHERIF, A. MINAGAWA, and J. WAHREN. Hypoglycemia during prolonged exercise in normal men. *N. Engl. J. Med.* 306:895-900, 1982.
12. FORDTRAN, J.A. and B. SALTIN. Gastric emptying and intestinal absorption during prolonged severe exercise. *J. Appl. Physiol.* 23:331-335, 1967.
13. GISOLFI, C.V. and J. COHEN. Relationships among training, heat acclimation and heat tolerance in men and women: the controversy revisited. *Med. Sci. Sports* 11:56-59, 1979.
14. GISOLFI, C.V. and J.R. COPPING. Thermal effects of prolonged treadmill exercise in the heat. *Med. Sci. Sports* 6:108-113, 1974.
15. HANSON, P.G. and S.W. ZIMMERMAN. Exertional heatstroke in novice runners. *JAMA* 242:154-157, 1979.
16. HART, L.E., B.P. EGIER, A.G. SHIMIZU, P.J. TANDON, and J.R. SUTTON. Exertional heat stroke: the runner's nemesis. *Can. Med. Assoc. J. 122: 1144-1150, 1980.*

17. HAYMES, E.M., R.J. McCORMICK, and E.R. BUSKIRK. Heat tolerance of exercising lean and obese prepubertal boys. *J. Appl. Physiol.* 39:457-461, 1975.

18. HUGHSON, R.L., H.J. GREEN, M.E. HOUSTON, J.A. THOMSON, D.R. MACLEAN, and J.R. SUTTON. Heat injuries in Canadian mass participation runs. *Can. Med. Assoc. J.* 122:1141-1144, 1980.

19. HUGHSON, R.L., L.A. STANDL, and J.M. MACKIE. Monitoring road racing in the heat. *Phys. Sportsmed.* 11(5):94-105, 1983.

20. KNOCHEL, J.P. Environmental heat illness: an eclectric review. *Arch. Intern. Med.* 133:841-864, 1974.

21. LEVINE, S.A., B. GORDON, and C.L. DERICK. Some changes in the chemical consituents of the blood following a marathon race. *JAMA* 82:1778-1779, 1924.

22. MARON, M.B., J.A. WAGNER, and S.M. HORVATH. Thermoregulatory responses during competitive distance running. *J. Appl. Physiol.* 42:909-914, 1977.

23. MAUGHAN, R.J., I.M. LIGHT, P.H. WHITING, and J.D.B. MILLER. Hypothermia, hyperkalemia, and marathon running. *Lancet* 11:1336, 1982.

24. NADEL, E.R. Control of sweating rate while exercising in the heat. *Med. Sci. Sports* 11:31-35, 1979.

25. NADEL, E.R., C.B. WENGER, M.F. ROBERTS, J.A.J. STOLWIJK, and E. CAFARELLI. Physiological defenses against hyperthermia of exercise. *Ann. NY Acad. Sci.* 301:98-109, 1977.

26. NOBLE, H.B. and D. BACHMAN. Medical aspects of distance race planning. *Phys. Sportsmed.* 7(6):78-84, 1979.

27. O'DONNELL, T.J., JR. Acute heatstroke. Epidemiologic, biochemical, renal and coagulation studies. *JAMA* 234:824-828, 1975.

28. PANDOLF, K.B., R.L. BURSE, and R.F. GOLDMAN. Role of physical fitness in heat acclimatization, decay and reinduction. *Ergonomics* 20:399-408, 1977.

29. PIWONKA, R.W., S. ROBINSON, V.L. GAY, and R.S. MANALIS. Preacclimatization of men to heat by training. *J. Appl. Physiol.* 20:379-384, 1965.

30. PUGH, L.G.C.E. Cold stress and muscular exercise with special reference to accidental hypothermia. *Br. Med. J.* 2:333-337, 1967.

31. PUGH, L.G.C.E., J.L. CORBETT, and R.H. JOHNSON. Rectal temperatures, weight losses and sweat rates in marathon running. *J. Appl. Physiol.* 23:347-352, 1967.

32. RICHARDS, D., R. RICHARDS, P.J. SCHOFIELD, V. ROSS, and J.R. SUTTON. Management of heat exhaustion in Sydney's *The Sun* City-to-Surf fun runners. *Med. J. Aust.* 2:457-461, 1979.

33. RICHARDS, R., D. RICHARDS, P.J. SCHOFIELD, V. ROSS, and J.R. SUTTON. Reducing the hazards in Sydney's *The Sun* City-to-Surf fun runs, 1971 to 1979. *Med. J. Aust.* 2:453-457, 1979.

34. RICHARDS, R., D. RICHARDS, P.J. SCHOFIELD, V. ROSS, and J.R. SUTTON. Organization of *The Sun* City-to-Surf fun run, Sydney, 1979. *Med. J. Aust.* 2:470-474, 1979.

35. ROBINSON, S., S.L. WILEY, L.G. BOUDURANT and S. MAMLIN, JR. Temperature regulation of men following heatstroke. *Isr. J. Med. Sci.* 12:786-795, 1976.

36. SHAPIRO, Y., A. MAGAZANIK, R. UDASSIN, G. BEN-BARUCH, E. SHVARTZ, and Y. SHOENFELD. Heat tolerance in former heatstroke patients. *Ann. Intern. Med.* 90:913-916, 1979.

37. SHIBOLET, S., R. COLL, T. GILAT, and E. SOHAR. Heatstroke: its clinical picture and mechanism in 36 cases. *Q.J. Med.* 36:525-547, 1967.

38. SHIBOLET, S., M.C. LANCASTER, and Y. DANON. Heat stroke: a review. *Aviat. Space Environ. Med.* 47:280-301, 1976.

39. SHVARTZ, E., Y. SHAPIRO, A. MAGAZANIK, et al. Heat acclimation, physical fitness, and responses to exercise in temperate and hot environments. *J. Appl. Physiol.* 43:678-683, 1977.

40. SUTTON, J. Community jogging vs. arduous racing. *N. Engl. J. Med.* 286:951, 1972.

41. SUTTON, J., M.J. COLEMAN, A.P. MILLAR, L. LAZARUS, and P. RUSSO. The medical problems of mass participation in athletic competition. The "City-to-Surf" race. *Med. J. Aust.* 2:127-133, 1972.

42. SUTTON, J.R. Heat illness. In: *Sports Medicine* R.H. Strauss (Ed.). Philadelphia: W.B. Saunders, 1984, pp. 307-322.

43. SUTTON, J.R. and O. BAR-OR. Thermal illness in fun running. *Am. Heart J.* 100:778-781, 1980.

44. THOMPSON, P.D., M.P. STERN, P. WILLIAMS, K. DUNCAN, W.L. HASKELL, and P.D. WOOD. Death during jogging or running. A study of 18 cases. *JAMA* 242:1265-1267, 1979.

45. WILLIAMS, R.S., D.D. SCHOCKEN, M. MOREY, and F.P. KOISCH. Medical aspects of competitive distance running. *Postgrad. Med.* 70:41-51, 1981.

46. WINSLOW, C.E.A., L.P. HERRINGTON, and A.P. GAGGE. Physiological reactions of the human body to various atmospheric humidities. *Am. J. Physiol.* 120:288-299, 1937.

47. WYNDHAM, C.H. and N.B. STRYDOM. The danger of inadequate water intake during marathon running. *S. Afr. Med. J.* 43:893-896, 1969.

48. YAGLOU, C.P. and D. MINARD. Control of heat casualties at military training centers. *AMA Arch. Ind. Health* 16:302-305, 1957.

References

Adams, T., & Heberling, E.J. (1958). Human physiological responses to a standardized cold stress as modified by physical fitness. *Journal of Applied Physiology, 13*, 226-230.

Adams, W.C., Bernauer, E.M., Dill, D.B., & Bomar, J.B. (1975). Effects of equivalent sea-level and altitude training on $\dot{V}O_2$max running and performance. *Journal of Applied Physiology, 39*, 262-266.

Adams, W.C., Savin, W.M., & Christ, A.E. (1981). Detection of ozone toxicity during continuous exercise via the effective dose concept. *Journal of Applied Physiology: Respiratory, Environmental, Exercise Physiology, 51*, 415-422.

Adolph, D.F. (1947). *Physiology of man in the desert.* New York: Interscience.

Adolph, E.F., & Molnar, G.W. (1946). Exchanges of heat and tolerances to cold in men exposed to outdoor weather. *American Journal of Physiology, 146*, 507-537.

American Academy of Pediatrics. (1983). Climatic heat stress in the exercising child. *The Physician and Sportsmedicine, 11*(8), 155, 159.

Andersen, I., Lundqvist, G.R., Jensen, P.L., & Proctor, D.F. (1974). Human response to controlled levels of sulfur dioxide. *Archives of Environmental Health, 26*, 156-160.

Andersen, K.L., Hart, J.S., Hammel, H.T., & Sabean, H.B. (1963). Metabolic and thermal responses of Eskimos during muscular exertion in the cold. *Journal of Applied Physiology, 18*, 613-618.

Arner, E.C., & Rhoades, R.A. (1973). Long-term nitrogen dioxide exposure, *Archives of Environmental Health, 26*, 156-160.

Aronow, W.S., Harris, C.N., Isbell, M.W., Rokaw, S.N., & Imparato, B. (1972). Effect of freeway travel on angina pectoris. *Annals of Internal Medicine, 77*, 669-676.

Asmussen, E., Bonde-Peterson, F., & Jorgensen, K. (1976). Mechano-elastic properties of human muscles at different temperatures. *Acta Physiologica Scandinavica, 96*, 83-93.

Åstrand, P.O. (1952). *Experimental studies of physical working capacity in relation to sex and age.* Copenhagen: Munksgaard.

Åstrand, P.O., & Rodahl, K. (1977). *Textbook of work physiology: Physiological bases of exercise* (2nd ed.). New York: McGraw Hill.

Åstrand, P.O., & Saltin, B. (1964). Plasma and red cell volume after prolonged severe exercise. *Journal of Applied Physiology, 19*, 829-832.

Bader, R.A., Eliot, J.W., & Bass, D.K. (1952). Hormonal and renal mechanisms of cold diuresis. *Journal of Applied Physiology, 4*, 649-658.

Balke, B. (1967). Summary of Magglingen Symposium on sports at medium altitude. In *The International Symposium on the Effects of Altitude on Physical Performance*. Chicago: The Athletic Institute.

Bar-Or, O. (1982). The child athlete and thermoregulation. In P.V. Komi (Ed.), *Exercise and Sport Biology*, International series on sport sciences (Vol. 12, pp. 127-134). Champaign, IL: Human Kinetics.

Bar-Or, O., Lundegren, H.M., & Buskirk, E.R. (1969). Heat tolerance of exercising lean and obese women. *Journal of Applied Physiology, 26*, 403-409.

Bar-Or, O., Shephard, R.J., & Allen, C.L. (1971). Cardiac output of 10- to 12-year-old boys and girls during submaximal exercise. *Journal of Applied Physiology, 30*, 219-233.

Baum, E., Bruck, K., & Schwennicke, H.P. (1976). Adaptive modifications in the thermoregulatory system of long-distance runners. *Journal of Applied Physiology, 40*, 404-410.

Bedi, J.F., Folinsbee, L.J., Horvath, S.M., & Ebenstein, R.S. (1979). Human exposure to sulfur dioxide and ozone: Absence of a synergistic effect. *Archives of Environmental Health, 38*, 233-239.

Bedi, J.F., Folinsbee, L.J., & Horvath, S.M. (1983). Pulmonary function changes of elite cyclists to 0.10 ppm ozone during exercise. *Medicine and Science in Sports and Exercise, 15*, 112.

Belding, H.S., Russel, H.D., Darling, R.C., & Folk, G.E. (1947). Analysis of factors concerned in maintaining energy expenditure for dressed men in extreme cold: Effects of activity on the protective value and comfort of the arctic uniform. *American Journal of Physiology, 149*, 223-239.

Benziner, T.H., Kinzinger, C., & Pratt, W.A. (1963). The human thermostat. In J.D. Hardy (Ed.), *Temperature: Its measurement and control in science and industry* (Vol. 3). New York: Reinhold.

Bergh, U., & Ekblom, B. (1979a). Influence of muscle temperature on maximal muscle strength and power output in human skeletal muscles. *Acta Physiologica Scandinavica, 107*, 33-37.

Bergh, U., & Ekblom, B. (1979b). Physical performance and peak aerobic power at different body temperatures. *Journal of Applied Physiology: Respiratory, Environmental, and Exercise Physiology, 46*, 885-889.

Bergh, U., Hartley, H., Landsberg, L., & Ekblom, B. (1979). Plasma norepinephrine concentration during submaximal and maximal exercise at lowered skin and core temperatures. *Acta Physiologica Scandinavica, 106*, 383-384.

Binkhorst, R.A., Hoofd, L., & Vissers, A.C.A. (1977). Temperature and force-velocity relationship of human muscles. *Journal of Applied Physiology: Respiratory, Environmental, and Exercise Physiology, 42*, 471-475.

Bodey, A.S. (1978). Changing cold acclimatization patterns of men living in Antarctica. *International Journal of Biometeorology, 22*, 163-176.

Buettner, K.J.K., & Slonin, N.B. (1974). Biometeorology. In N. Balfour Slonin (Ed.), *Environmental physiology*, St. Louis: C.V. Mosby Co.

Buick, F.J., Gledhill, N., Froese, A.B., & Spriet, L.L. (1982). Red cell mass and aerobic performance at sea level. In J.R. Sutton, N.L. Jones & C.S. Huston (Eds.), *Hypoxia: Man at altitude*. New York: Thieme-Statton Inc.

Bullard, R.W., Banerjee, M.R., Chen, F., Elizondo, R., & MacIntyre, B.A. (1968). The influence of skin temperature on the rate of eccrine sweating. Air Force Office of Scientific Research contract F44620-68-C-0014, and U.S. Army Medical Corps contract 17-68-C-8060.

Bullard, R.W., Banerjee, M.R., & MacIntyre. B.A. (1967). The role of the skin in negative feedback regulation of eccrine sweating. *International Journal of Biometeorology, 11*, 93-104.

Bundschuh, E.L., & Clarke, D.H. (1982). Muscle responses to maximal fatiguing exercise in cold water. *American Corrective Therapy Journal, 36*, 82-87.

Burton, A.C., & Edholm, O.G. (1955). *Man in a cold environment*. London: Edward Arnold Publishers Ltd.

Buskirk, E.R., & Grasley, W.C. (1968). Heat injury and conduct of athletes. In *Physiological aspects of sports and physical fitness*. Chicago: Athletic Institute.

Buskirk, E.R., Kollias, J. Akers, R.F., Prokop, E.K., & Picon-Reatigue, E.P. (1967a). Maximal performance at altitude and on return from altitude in conditioned runners. *Journal of Applied Physiology, 23* 259-266.

Buskirk, E.R., Kollias, J., Picon-Reatigue, E., Akers, R., Prokop, E., & Baker, P. (1967b). Physiology and performance of track athletes at various altitudes in the United States and Peru. In *The International Symposium on the Effects of Altitude on Physical Performance*. Chicago: The Athletic Institute.

Buskirk, E.R., Loomis, J.L., & McLaughlin, E.R. (1971). Microclimate over artificial turf. *National Association of College Directors Athletic Quarterly, 5*, 22-24.

Buskirk, E.R., Thompson, R.H., & Whedon, G.D. (1963). Metabolic response to cold air in men and women in relation to total body fat content. *Journal of Applied Physiology, 18*, 603-612.

Cabanac, M. (1975). Temperature regulation. *Annual Review of Physiology, 37*, 415-439.

Cabanac, M., & Caputa, M. (1979). Open loop increase in trunk temperature produced by face cooling in working humans. *Journal of Physiology, 289*, 163-174.

Carlson, L., & Hsieh, A.C.L. (1974). Temperature and humidity, Part A: Cold. In N. Balfour Slonin (Ed.), *Environmental physiology*. St. Louis: C.V. Mosby Co.

Carlson, L.D., Hsieh, A.C.L., Fullington, F., & Elsner, R.W. (1958). Immersion in cold water and body tissue insulation. *Journal of Aviation Medicine, 29*, 145-152.

Clarke, R.S.J., Hellon, R.F., & Lind, A.R. (1958). The duration of sustained contractions of the human forearm at different muscle temperatures. *Journal of Physiology, 143*, 454-473.

Colin, J., Timbal, J., Guieu, J., Boutelier, C., & Houdas, Y. (1970). Combined effect of radiation and convection. In J.D. Hardy, A.P. Gagge, & J.A.J. Stolwijk (Eds.), *Physiological and behavioral temperature regulation*. Springfield: Charles C. Thomas.

Comroe, J.H. (1974). *Physiology of respiration* (2nd ed.). Chicago: Year Book Medical Publishers.

Consolazio, C.F., Johnson, H.L., & Krzywicki, H.J. (1972). Body fluids, body composition, and metabolic aspect of high-altitude adaptation. In M.K. Yousef, S.M. Horvath, & R.W. Bullard (Eds.), *Physiological adaptations: Desert and mountain*. New York: Academic Press.

Consolazio, C.F., Matoush, L.O., Johnson, H.L., Krzywicki, H.J., Daws, T.A., & Isaac, G.J. (1969). Effects of high-carbohydrate diets on performance and clinical symptomatology after rapid ascent to high altitude. *Federation Proceedings, 28*, 937-943.

Copes, K., & Rosentswieg, J. (1972). The effects of sleep deprivation upon motor performance of ninth-grade students. *Journal of Sports Medicine and Physical Fitness, 12*, 47-53.

Costill, D.L. (1980). Fluids for athletic performance: Why and what should you drink during prolonged exercise? In E.J. Burke (Ed.), *Toward an understanding of human performance* (2nd ed., pp. 130-140). New York: Mouvement Publications.

Costill, D.L., Kammer, W.F., & Fisher, A. (1970). Fluid ingestion during distance running. *Archives of Environmental Health, 21*, 520-525.

Costill, D.L., & Saltin, B. (1974). Factors limiting gastric emptying during rest and exercise. *Journal of Applied Physiology, 37*, 679-683.

Costill, D.L., & Sparks, K.E. (1973). Rapid fluid replacement following thermal dehydration. *Journal of Applied Physiology, 34*, 299-303.

Coyle, E.F., Costill, D.L., Fink, W.J., & Hoopes, D.C. (1978). Gastric emptying rates for selected athletic drinks. *Research Quarterly, 49*, 119-124.

Craig, A.B. (1969). Olympics 1968: A post-mortem. *Medicine and Science in Sports, 1*, 177-180.

Craig, A.B., & Dvorak, M. (1969). Comparison of exercise in air and in water of different temperatures. *Medicine and Science in Sports, 1*, 124-130.

Daniels, J., & Oldridge, N. (1970). The effects of alternate exposure to altitude and sea level on world-class middle-distance runners. *Medicine and Science in Sports, 2*, 107-112.

Davies, C.T.M., Mecrow, I.K., & White, M.J. (1982). Contractile properties of the human triceps surae with some observations on the effects of temperature and exercise. *European Journal of Applied Physiology, 49*, 255-269.

Davies, M., Ekblom, B., Bergh, U., & Kanstrup-Jensen, I.L. (1975). The effects of hypothermia on submaximal and maximal work performance. *Acta Physiologica Scandinavica, 95*, 201-202.

Davies, T.R.A. (1961). Chamber cold acclimatization in man. *Journal of Applied Physiology, 16*, 1011-1015.

Davies, T.R.A., & Johnston, D.R. (1961). Seasonal acclimatization to cold in man. *Journal of Applied Physiology, 16*, 231-234.

DeGraff, A.C., Grover, R.F., Johnson, R.L., Hammond, J.W., & Miller, J.M. (1970). Diffusing capacity of the lung in Caucasians native to 3,100 m. *Journal of Applied Physiology, 29*, 71-76.

Dempsey, J.A., Reddan, W.G., Birnbaum, M.L., Foster, H.V., Thoden, J.S., Grover, R.F., & Rankin, J. (1971). Effects of acute through life-long hypoxic exposure on exercise pulmonary gas exchange. *Respiration Physiology, 13*, 62-89.

Dill, D.B., Yousef, M.K., & Nelson, J.D. (1973). Responses of men and women to two-hour walks in the desert heat. *Journal of Applied Physiology, 35*, 231-235.

Drinkwater, B.L., Kupprat, I.C., Denton, J.E., Crist, J.L., & Horvath, S.M. (1977). Response of prepubertal girls and college women to work in the heat. *Journal of Applied Physiology, 43*, 1046-1053.

Drinkwater, B.L., Raven, P.B., Horvath, S.M., Gliner, J.A., Ruhling, R.O., Bolduan, N.W., & Taguchi, S. (1974). Air pollution, exercise, and heat stress. *Archives of Environmental Health, 28*, 177-181.

Edwards, R.H.T., Harris, R.C., Hultman, E., Kaijser, L., Koh, D., & Nordesjo, L-O. (1972). Effect of temperature on muscle energy metabolism and endurance during successive isometric contraction, sustained to fatigue, of the quadriceps muscle in man. *Journal of Physiology*, **220**, 335-352.

Ehret, C.F., Groh, K.R., & Meinert, J.C. (1980). Considerations of diet in allieviating jet lag. In L.E. Scheving & F. Halberg (Eds.), *Principles and applications to shifts in schedules* (pp. 393-402). Rockville, MD: Sijthoff & Noordhoff.

Ehret, C.F., & Scanlon, L.W. (1983). *Overcoming jet lag.* New York: Berkley.

Ekblom, B., Huot, R., Stein, E.M., & Thorstensson, A.T. (1975). Effect of changes in arterial oxygen content on circulation and physical performance. *Journal of Applied Physiology*, **39**, 71-75.

Environmental Criteria and Assessment Office. (1979). *Air quality criteria for carbon monoxide.* Washington: U.S. Environmental Protection Agency.

Environmental Criteria and Assessment Office. (1982). *Air quality criteria for particulate matter and sulfur oxides.* Washington: U.S. Environmental Protection Agency.

Faulkner, J.A., Kollias, J., Favour, C.B., Buskirk, E.R., & Balke, B. (1967). Maximum aerobic capacity and running performance at altitude. In *The International Symposium on the Effects of Altitude on Physical Performance.* Chicago: The Athletic Institute.

Faulkner, J.A., Kollias, J., Favour, C.B., Buskirk, E.R., & Balke, B. (1968). Maximum aerobic capacity and running performance at altitude. *Journal of Applied Physiology*, **24**, 685-691.

Fink, W.J., Costill, D.L., & Van Handel, P.J. (1975). Leg muscle metabolism during exercise in the heat and cold. *European Journal of Applied Physiology*, **34**, 183-190.

Folinsbee, L.J., Bedi, J.F., & Horvath, S.M. (1980). Respiratory responses in humans repeatedly exposed to low concentrations of ozone. *American Review of Respiratory Disease*, **121**, 431-439.

Folinsbee, L.J., Drinkwater, B.L., Bedi, J.F., & Horvath, S.M. (1978). The influence of exercise on the pulmonary function changes due to exposure to low concentrations of ozone. In L.J. Folinsbee, J.A. Wagner, J.F. Borgla, B.L. Drinkwater, J.A. Gliner, & J.F. Bedi (Eds.), *Environmental stress: Individual human adaptations.* New York: Academic Press.

Folinsbee, L.J., Horvath, S.M., Bedi, J.F., & Delehunt, J.C. (1978). Effect of 0.62 ppm NO_2 on cardiopulmonary function in young male nonsmokers. *Environmental Research*, **15**, 199-205.

Folinsbee, L.J., Horvath, S.M., Raven, P.B., Bedi, J.F., Morton, A.R., Drinkwater, B.L., Bolduan, N.W., & Gliner, J.A. (1977). Influence of exercise and heat stress on pulmonary function during ozone exposure. *Journal of Applied Physiology: Respiratory, Environmental, Exercise Physiology*, **43**, 409-413.

Folinsbee, L.J., Silverman, F., & Shephard, R.J. (1977). Decrease of maximum work performance allowing ozone exposure. *Journal of Applied Physiology: Respiratory, Environmental, Exercise Physiology*, 531-536.

Folk, C.E. (1974). *Textbook of environmental physiology* (pp. 87-132, 218-277). Philadelphia: Lea & Febiger.

Fox, E.L., & Mathews, D.K. (1981). *The physiological basis of physical education and athletics* (3rd ed., p. 475). Philadelphia: Saunders College Publishing.

Frisancho, A.R. (1979). *Human adaptation: A functional interpretation* (pp. 11-26). St. Louis: C.V. Mosby Co.

Froese, G., & Burton, A.C. (1957). Heat loss from the human head. *Journal of Applied Physiology*, **10**, 235-241.

Galbo, H., Houston, M.E., Christensen, N.J., Holst, J.J., Nielsen, B., Nygaard, E., & Suzuki, J. (1979). The effect of water temperature on the hormonal response to prolonged swimming. *Acta Physiologica Scandinavica*, **105**, 326-337.

Gliner, J.A., Horvath, S.M., & Mihevic, P.M. (1983). Carbon monoxide and human performance in a single and dual task methodology. *Aviation, Space, and Environmental Medicine*, **54**, 714-717.

Gliner, J.A., Raven, P.B., Horvath, S.M., Drinkwater, B.L., & Sutton, J.C. (1975). Man's physiologic response to long-term work during thermal and pollutant stress. *Journal of Applied Physiology*, **39**, 628-632.

Goddard, R.F., & Favour, C.B. (1967). United States Olympic committee swimming team performance in international sports week, Mexico City, 1965. In *The International Symposium on the Effects of Altitude on Physical Performance*. Chicago: The Athletic Institute.

Goldsmith, J.R., & Landaw, S.A. (1968). Carbon monoxide and human health. *Science*, **162**, 1352-1359.

Graeber, R.C. (1980). Recent studies relative to the airlifting of military units across time zones. In L.E. Scheving, & F. Halberg (Eds.), *Principles and applications of shifts of schedules* (pp. 353-369). Rockville, MD: Sijthoff & Noordhoff.

Graham, T.E., (1981). Thermal and glycemic responses during mild exercise in $+5$ to -15 C environments following alcohol injestion. *Aviation, Space, and Environmental Medicine*, **52**, 517-522.

Graham, T.E. (1983). Alcohol ingestion and sex differences on the thermal responses to mild exercise in a cold environment, *Human Biology*, **55**, 463-476.

Greenleaf, J.E., Bernauer, E.M., Adams, W.E., & Juhos, L. (1978). Fluid-electrolyte shifts and $\dot{V}O_2$max in man at simulated altitude (2,287 m). *Journal of Applied Physiology: Respiratory, Environmental, and Exercise Physiology*, **44**, 652-658.

Grover, R.F. (1978). Adaptation to high altitude. In L.J. Folinsbee, J.A. Wagner, J.F. Borgia, B.L. Drinkwater, J.A. Gliner, & J.F. Bedi (Eds.), *Environmental stress: Individual human adaptations*. New York: Academic Press.

Grover, R.F., & Reeves, J.T. (1967) Exercise performance of athletes at sea level and 3,100 meters altitude. In *The International Symposium on the Effects of Altitude on Physical Performance*. Chicago: The Athletic Institute.

Haagen-Smith, A.J. (1966). Carbon monoxide levels in city driving. *Archives of Environmental Health*, **12**, 548-551.

Hackett, P.H., Rennie, D., & Levine, H.D. (1976). The incidence, importance, and prophylaxis of acute mountain sickness. *Lancet*, **II**, 1149-1154.

Hackney, J.D., Linn, W.S., Mohler, J.G., & Collier, C.R. (1977b). Adaptation to short-term respiratory effects of ozone in men exposed repeatedly. *Journal of Applied Physiology: Respiratory, Environmental, Exercise Physiology*, **43**, 82-85.

Hackney, J.D., Linn, W.S., Karuza, S.K., Buckley, R.D., Law, D.C., Bates, D.V., Hazucha, M., Pengelly, L.D., & Silverman, F. (1977a). Effects of ozone exposure in Canadians and southern Californians. *Archives of Environmental Health*, **32**, 110-116.

Hackney, J.D., Linn, W.S., Buckley, R.D., Collier, C.R., & Mohler, J.G. (1978). Respiratory and biochemical adaptations in men repeatedly exposed to ozone. In L.J.

Follinsbee, J.A. Wagner, J.F. Borgia, B.L. Drinkwater, & J.F. Bedi (Eds.), *Environmental stress: Individual human adaptations*. New York: Academic Press.

Haight, J.S.J., & Keatinge, W.R. (1973). Failure of thermoregulation in the cold during hypoglycaemia induced by exercise and ethanol. *Journal of Physiology, 229*, 87-97.

Hall, J.F., & Polte, J.W. (1956). Effect of water content and compression on clothing insulation. *Journal of Applied Physiology, 8*, 530-545.

Hanna, J.M., & Hong, S.K. (1972). Critical water temperature and effective insulation in scuba divers in Hawaii. *Journal of Applied Physiology, 33*, 770-773.

Hannon, J.P. (1978). Comparative altitude adaptability of young men and women. In L.J. Folinsbee, J.A. Wagner, J.F. Borgia, B.L. Drinkwater, J.A. Gliner, & J.F. Bedi (Eds.), *Environmental stress: Individual human adaptations*. New York; Academic Press.

Hannon, J.P., Klain, G.J., Sudman, D.M., & Sullivan, F.J. (1976). Nutritional aspects of high-altitude exposure in women. *American Journal of Clinical Nutrition, 29*, 604-613.

Hardy, J.D. (1965). The "set-point" concept in physiological temperature regulation. In W.S. Yamamoto & J.R. Brobeck (Eds.), *Physiological controls and regulation*. Philadelphia: W.B. Saunders.

Hardy, J.D. (1967). Central and peripheral factors in physiological temperature regulation. In *Les concepts de Claude Bernard sur le milieu interieur* (p. 247). Paris: Masson et Cie.

Haymes, E.M., & Buskirk, E.R. (1980). Prevention of heat injuries. In G.A. Stull (Ed.), *Encyclopedia of Physical Education, Fitness, and Sports: Training, Environment, Nutrition, and Fitness* (pp. 139-149). Salt Lake City: Brighton Publishing Co.

Haymes, E.M., Buskirk, E.R., Hodgson, J.L., Lundegren, H.M., & Nicholas, W.C. (1974). Heat tolerance of exercising lean and heavy prepubertal girls. *Journal of Applied Physiology, 36*, 566-571.

Haymes, E.M., Cartee, G.D., Rape, S.M., Garcia, E.S., & Temples, T.E. (1982). Thermal and metabolic responses of men and women during exercise in cold and neutral environments. *Medicine and Science in Sports and Exercise, 14*, 126.

Haymes, E.M., & Dickinson, A.L. (1978). Heat loss: Clothing and wind. *Journal of the United States Ski Coaches Association, 2*, 96-103.

Haymes, E.M., Dickinson, A.L., Malville, N., & Ross, R.W. (1982). Effects of wind on the thermal and metabolic responses to exercise in the cold. *Medicine and Science in Sports and Exercise, 14*, 41-45.

Haymes, E.M., McCormick, R.J., & Buskirk, E.R. (1975). Heat tolerance of exercising lean and obese boys. *Journal of Applied Physiology, 39*, 257-261.

Hayward, J.S., Collis, M., & Eckerson, J.D. (1973). Thermographic evaluation of relative heat loss areas of man during cold water immersion. *Aerospace Medicine, 44*, 708-711.

Hayward, J.S., Eckerson, J.D., & Collis, M.L. (1975). Thermal balance and survival time prediction of man in cold water. *Canadian Journal of Physiology and Pharmacology, 52*, 21-32.

Hazucha, M., & Bates, D.V. (1975). Combined effect of ozone and sulfur dioxide on human pulmonary function. *Nature, 257*, 50-51.

Henschel, A.F. (1974). Environmental pollution. In N.B. Slonin (Ed.), *Environmental physiology.* St. Louis: C.V. Mosby.

Herbert, W.G. (1980). Water and physical performance. In G.A. Stull (Ed.), *Encyclopedia of Physical Education, Fitness, and Sports: Training, Environment, Nutrition, and Fitness* (pp. 150-160). Salt Lake City: Brighton Publishing Co.

Holmer, I., & Bergh, U. (1974). Metabolic and thermal response to swimming in water at varying temperatures. *Journal of Applied Physiology, 37*, 702-705.

Hong, S-I., & Nadel, E.R. (1979). Thermogenic control during exercise in a cold environment. *Journal of Applied Physiology: Respiratory, Environmental, and Exercise Physiology, 47*, 1084-1089.

Hong, S.K. (1973). Pattern of cold adaptation in women divers of Korea (ama). *Federation Proceedings, 32*, 1614-1622.

Hong, S.K., Lee, C.K., Kim, J.K., Song, S.H., & Rennie, D.W. (1969). Peripheral blood flow and heat flux of Korean women divers. *Federation Proceedings, 28*, 1143-1148.

Horstman, D., Weiskopf, R., & Jackson, R.E. (1980). Work capacity during 3-wk sojourn at 4,300 m: Effects of relative polycythemia. *Journal of Applied Physiology: Respiratory, Environmental, and Exercise Physiology, 49*, 311-318.

Horvath, S.M. (1948). Reactions of men exposed to cold and wind. *American Journal of Physiology, 152*, 242-249.

Horvath, S.M. (1981). Historical perspectives of adaptation to heat. In S.M. Horvath & M.K. Yousef (Eds.), *Environmental physiology: Aging, heat, and altitude* (pp. 11-25). New York: Elsevier/North Holland.

Horvath, S.M. (1982). Impact of air quality on exercise performance. In D.I. Miller (Ed.), *Exercise and sport sciences reviews* (Vol. 9). Philadelphia: The Franklin Institute.

Horvath, S.M., Raven, P.B., Dahms, T.E., & Gray, D.J. (1975). Maximal aerobic capacity at different levels of carboxyhemoglobin. *Journal of Applied Physiology, 38*, 300-303.

Hultgren, H.N. (1982). High altitude medical problems. In J.R. Sutton, N.L. Jones & C.S. Houston (Eds.), *Hypoxia: Man at altitude.* New York: Thieme-Stratton Inc.

Hurley, B.F., & Haymes, E. (1982). The effects of rest and exercise in the cold on substrate mobilization and utilization. *Aviation, Space, and Environmental Medicine, 53*, 1193-1197.

Inbar, Omri. (1978). *Acclimatization to dry and hot environment in young adults and children 8-10 years old.* Ph.D. dissertation, Columbia University, New York, New York.

Ingram, D.L., & Mount, L.E. (1975). *Man and animals in hot environments.* New York: Springer Verlag.

Joy, R.J.T. (1963). Responses of cold-acclimatized men to infused norepinephrine. *Journal of Applied Physiology, 18*, 1209-1212.

Kang, B.S., Han, D.S., Paik, K.S., Park, Y.S., Kim, J.K., Kim, C.S., Rennie, D.W., & Hong, S.K. (1970). Calorigenic action of norepinephrine in the Korean women divers. *Journal of Applied Physiology, 29*, 6-9.

Kaufman, W.C. (1982). Cold-weather clothing for comfort or heat conservation. *The Physician and Sportsmedicine, 10*(2), 71-75.

Kaufman, W.C. (1983). The hand and foot in the cold. *The Physician and Sportsmedicine, 11*(2), 156-168.

Kaufman, W.C., Bothe, D., & Meyer, S.D. (1982). Thermal insulation capabilities and outdoor clothing materials. *Science, 215*, 690-191.

Kawahata, A. (1960). Sex differences in sweating. In J. Yoshimura et al., (Eds.), *Essential problems in climatic physiology* (pp. 169-184). Kyoto, Japan: Nankada Publishing Co., Ltd.

Keatinge, W.R. (1969). *Survival in cold water.* Oxford: Blackwell Scientific Publications.

Keatinge, W.R. (1961). The effect of repeated daily exposure to cold and of improved physical fitness on the metabolic and vascular response to cold air. *Journal of Physiology,* **157,** 209-220.

Klein, K.E., & Wegmann, H.M. (1980). The effect of transmeridian and transequatorial air travel on psychological well-being and performance. In L.E. Scheving & F. Halberg (Eds.), *Principles and applications to shifts in schedule* (pp. 339-352). Rockville, MD: Sijthoff & Noordhof.

Knuttgen, H.G., & Saltin, B., (1973). Oxygen uptake, muscle high-energy phosphates, and lactate in exercise under acute hypoxic conditions in man. *Acta Physiologica Scandinavica,* **87,** 368-376.

Koenig, J.Q., Pierson, W.E., & Frank, R. (1980). Acute effects of inhaled SO_2 plus NaCl droplet aerosol on pulmonary function in asthmatic adolescents. *Environmental Research,* **22,** 145-153.

Koenig, J.Q., Pierson, W.E., Horike, M., & Frank, R. (1982). Effects of inhaled sulfur dioxide (SO_2) on pulmonary function in healthy adolescents: Exposure to SO_2 alone or SO_2 + sodium chloride droplet aerosol during rest and exercise. *Archives of Environmental Health,* **37,** 5-9.

Koenig, J.Q., Pierson, W.E., Horike, M., & Frank, R. (1981). Effects of SO_2 plus NaCl aerosol with moderate exercise on pulmonary function in asthmatic adolescents. *Environmental Research,* **25,** 340-348.

Kollias, J., & Buskirk, E.R. (1974). Exercise and altitude. In W.R. Johnson & E.R. Buskirk (Eds.), *Science and medicine of exercise and sport* (2nd ed.). New York: Harper & Row.

Kollias, J., Barlett, L., Bergsteinova, V., Skinner, J.S., Buskirk, E.R., & Nicholas, W.C. (1974). Metabolic and thermal responses of women during cooling in water. *Journal of Applied Physiology,* **36,** 577-580.

Kollias, J., Boileau, R., & Buskirk, E.R. (1972). Effects of physical conditioning in man on thermal responses to cold air. *International Journal of Biometeorology,* **16,** 389-402.

Korcok, M. (1981). Summer Olympics to be under ozone cloud. *Journal of the American Medical Association,* **246,** 202.

Kramar, P.O., Drinkwater, B.L., Folinsbee, L.J., & Bedi, J.F. (1983). Ocular functions and incidence of acute mountain sickness in women at altitude. *Aviation, Space, and Environmental Medicine,* **54,** 116-120.

Kuno, Y. (1956). *Human perspiration.* Springfield, Illinois: Charles C. Thomas.

Lamb, D.R. (1978). *Physiology of exercise: Responses and adaptations.* New York: Macmillan Publishing Co.

Lebowitz, M.D., Bendheim, P., Cristea, G., Markowitz, D., Misiaszek, J., Staniec, M., & Van Wyck, D. (1974). The effect of air pollution and weather on lung function in exercising children and adolescents. *American Review of Respiratory Disease,* **109,** 262-273.

Lenfant, C., Torrance, J., English, E., Finch, C.A., Reynafarje, C., Ramos, J., & Faura, J. (1968). Effect of altitude on oxygen binding by hemoglobin and on organic phosphate levels. *Journal of Clinical Investigation,* **47,** 2652.

Lewis, T. (1930). Observations upon reactions of vessels of human skin to cold. *Heart, 15*, 177-208.

Linn, W.S., Jones, M.P., Bailey, R.M., Kleinman, M.T., Spier, C.E., Fischer, D.A., & Hackney, J.D. (1980). Respiratory effects of mixed nitrogen dioxide and sulfur dioxide in human volunteers under simulated ambient exposure conditions. *Environmental Research, 22*, 431-438.

Lippman, M., Albert, R.E., Yeates, D.B., Wales, K., & Leikauf, G. (1980). Effect of sulfuric acid mist on mucociliary bronchial clearance in healthy nonsmoking humans. *Journal of Aerosol Science, 247.*

Luce, G.G. (1971). *Body time.* New York: Bantam Books.

Marshall, H.C. (1972). The effects of cold exposure and exercise upon peripheral function. *Archives of Environmental Health, 24*, 325-330.

Martin, B.J. (1981). Effect of sleep deprivation on tolerance of prolonged exercise. *European Journal of Applied Physiology, 47*, 345-354.

Martin, B.J., & Chen, H-I. (1984). Sleep loss and the sympathoadrenal response to exercise. *Medicine and Science in Sports and Exercise, 16*, 56-59.

McArdle, W.E., Magel, J.R., Lesmes, G.R., & Pechar, G.S. (1976). Metabolic and cardiovascular adjustment to work in air and water at 18, 25, and 33 C. *Journal of Applied Physiology, 40*, 85-90.

McCafferty, W.B. (1981). *Air pollution and athletic performance.* Springfield: Charles C. Thomas.

McCafferty, W.B., Clamp, C.D., Straker, J.S., & Fee, R.F. (1979). Oxidant air pollution and athletic training. *Abstracts of Research Papers 1979 AAHPER Convention, 133.*

McFarland, R.A. (1972). Psychophysiological implications of life at altitude and including the role of oxygen in the process of aging. In M.K. Yousef, S.M. Horvath & R.W. Bullard (Eds.), *Physiological adaptations: Desert and mountain.* New York: Academic Press.

McMurray, R.G., & Horvath, S.M. (1979). Thermoregulation in swimmers and runners. *Journal of Applied Physiology: Respiratory, Environmental, and Exercise Physiology, 46*, 1086-1092.

Melton, C.E. (1982). Effects of long-term exposure to low levels of ozone: A review. *Aviation, Space, and Environmental Medicine, 53*, 105-111.

Nadel, E.R., Holmer, I., Bergh, U., Åstrand, P.O., & Stolwijk, J.A.J. (1974). Energy exchanges of swimming man. *Journal of Applied Physiology, 36*, 465-471.

Nadel, E.R., Holmer, I., Bergh, U., Åstrand, P.O., & Stolwijk J.A.J. (1973). Thermoregulatory shivering during exercise. *Life Sciences, 13*, 983-989.

Nicholson, J.P., & Case, D.B. (1983). Carboxyhemoglobin levels in New York City runners. *The Physician and Sportsmedicine, 11*(3), 135-138.

Nielsen, B. (1976). Metabolic reactions to changes in core and skin temperature in man. *Acta Physiologica Scandinavica, 97*, 129-138.

Nishi, Y., & Gagge, A.P. (1970). Direct evaluation of convective heat transfer by naphthalene sublimation. *Journal of Applied Physiology, 29*, 830-838.

Office of the Federal Register: National Archives and Records Service. (1983). *Code of Federal Regulations: Protection of Environment.* Washington: General Services Administration.

Office of Research and Development. (1978). *Air Quality Criteria for Ozone and Other Photochemical Oxidants* (Vol. 1) Washington: U.S. Environmental Protection Agency.

O'Hara, W.J., Allen, C., Shephard, R.J., & Allen, G. (1979). Fat loss in the cold—a controlled study. *Journal of Applied Physiology: Respiratory, Environmental, and Exercise Physiology,* **46**, 872-877.

O'Hara, W.J., Allen, C., & Shephard, R.J. (1977a). Loss of body fat during an arctic winter expedition. *Canadian Journal of Physiology and Pharmacology,* **55**, 1235-1241.

O'Hara, W.J., Allen, C., & Shephard, R.J. (1977b). Loss of body weight and fat during exercise in a cold chamber. *European Journal of Applied Physiology,* **37**, 205-218.

Paolone, A.M., Wells, C.L., & Kelly, G.T. (1977). Sexual variations in thermoregulation during heat stress. *Aviation, Space, and Environmental Medicine,* **49**, 715-719.

Park, Y.S., Rennie, D.W., Lee, I.S., Park, Y.D., Paik, K.S., Kang, D.H., Suh, D.J., Lee, S.H., Hong, S.Y., & Hong, S.K. (1983). Time course of deacclimatization to cold water immersion in Korean women divers. *Journal of Applied Physiology: Respiratory, Environmental, Exercise Physiology,* **54**, 1708-1716.

Peterson, J.E., & Stewart, R.D. (1970). Absorption and elimination of carbon monoxide by inactive young men. *Archives of Environmental Health,* **21**, 165-171.

Pickett, G.F., & Morris, A.F. (1975). Effects of acute sleep and food deprivation on total body response time and cardiovascular performance. *Journal of Sports Medicine and Physical Fitness,* **15**, 49-53.

Pirnay, F., Dujardin, J., Deroanne, R., & Petit, J.M. (1971). Muscular exercise during intoxication by carbon monoxide. *Journal of Applied Physiology,* **31**, 573-575.

Pitts, G.C., Johnson, R.E., & Consolazio, F.C. (1944). Work in the heat as affected by intake of water, salt and glucose. *American Journal of Physiology,* **142**, 253-259.

Prevention of thermal injuries during distance running. Position Statement of the American College of Sports Medicine. (1984). *Sports Medicine Bulletin,* **19**(3), 3-12.

Prosser, C.L. (1964). Perspectives of adaptation: Theoretical aspects. In *Handbook of physiology, Section 4, Adaptation to the environment* (pp. 11-25), D.B. Dill et al. (Eds.) American Physiological Society.

Pugh, L.G.C.E. (1958). Muscular exercise on Mount Everest. *Journal of Physiology,* **141**, 233-261.

Pugh, L.G.C.E. (1964a). Animals at high altitudes: Man above 5,000 meters-mountain exploration. In *Handbook of physiology, Section 4, Adaptation to the environment.* D.B. Dill et al. (Eds.) American Physiological Society.

Pugh, L.G.C.E. (1964b). Deaths from exposure on Four Inns walking competition, March 14-15, 1964. *Lancet,* **1**, 1210-1212.

Pugh, L.G.C.E. (1966a). Accidental hypothermia in walkers, climbers, and campers: Report to the medical commission on accident prevention. *British Medical Journal,* **1**, 123-129.

Pugh, L.G.C.E. (1966b). Clothing insulation and accidental hypothermia in youth. *Nature,* **209**, 1281-1286.

Pugh, L.G.C.E. (1967a). Athletes at altitude. *Journal of Physiology,* **192**, 619-646.

Pugh, L.G.C.E. (1967b). Cold stress and muscular exercise, with special reference to accidental hypothermia. *British Medical Journal,* **2**, 333-337.

Pugh, L.G.C.E. (1970). Oxygen intake in track and treadmill running with observations on the effect of air resistance. *Journal of Physiology,* **207**, 823-835.

Pugh, L.G.C.E., Corbett, J.L., & Johnson, R.H. (1967). Rectal temperature, weight losses and sweat rates in marathon running. *Journal of Applied Physiology,* **23**, 347-352.

Pugh, L.G.C.E., & Edholm, O.G. (1955). The physiology of channel swimmers. *Lancet,* **269**, 761-768.

Pugh, L.G.C.E., Gill, M.B., Lahiri, S., Milledge, J.S., Ward, M.P., & West, J.B. (1964). Muscular exercise at great altitudes. *Journal of Applied Physiology,* **19**, 431-440.

Raven, P.B., Drinkwater, B.L., Horvath, S.M., Ruhling, R.O., Gliner, J.A., Sutton, J.C., & Bolduan, N.W. (1974). Age, smoking habits, heat stress, and their interactive effects with carbon monoxide and peroxyacetylnitrate on man's aerobic power. *International Journal of Biometeorology,* **18**, 222-232.

Raven, P.B., Gliner, J.A., & Sutton, J.C. (1976). Dynamic lung function changes following long-term work in polluted environments. *Environmental Research,* **12**, 18-25.

Raven, P.B., Niki, I., Dahms, T.E., & Horvath, S.M. (1970). Compensatory cardiovascular responses during an environmental cold stress, 5 C. *Journal of Applied Physiology,* **29**, 417-421.

Rennie, D.W., Park, Y., Veicsteinas, A., & Pendergast, D. (1980). Metabolic and circulatory adaptation to cold water stress. In P. Cerretelli & B.J. Whipp (Eds.), *Exercise bioenergetics and gas exchange* (pp. 315-321). Amsterdam: Elsevier/North Holland Biomedical Press.

Reynafarje, C., Lozano, R., & Valdiviesto, J. (1959). The polycythemia of high altitudes: Iron metabolism and related aspects. *Blood,* **14**, 433-455.

Riggs, C.E., Johnson, D.J., Kilgour, R.D., Konopka, B.J. (1983). Metabolic effects of facial cooling in exercise. *Aviation, Space, and Environmental Medicine,* **54**, 22-26.

Robertson, R.J., Glicher, R., Metz, K.F., Skrinar, G.S., Allison, T.G., Bahnson, H.T., Abbott, R.A., Becker, R., & Falkel, J.E. (1982). Effect of induced erythrocythemia on hypoxia tolerance during physical exercise. *Journal of Applied Physiology: Respiratory, Environmental, Exercise Physiology,* **53**, 490-495.

Rochelle, R.D., & Horvath, S.M. (1978). Thermoregulation in surfers and nonsurfers immersed in cold water. *Undersea Biomedical Research,* **5**, 377-390.

Sackner, M.A., Ford, D., Fernandez, R., Cipley. J., Perez, J., Kwoka, M., Reinhart, M., Michaelson, E.D., Schreck, R., & Wanner, A. (1978). Effects of sulfuric acid aerosol on cardiopulmonary function of dogs, sheep, and humans. *American Review of Respiratory Disease,* **118**, 497-510.

Saltin, B. (1964). Aerobic and anaerobic work capacity after dehydration. *Journal of Applied Physiology,* **19**, 1114-1118.

Saltin, B. (1967). Aerobic and anaerobic work capacity at an altitude of 2,250 meters. In *The International Symposium on the Effects of Altitude on Physical Performance.* Chicago: The Athletic Institute.

Saltin, B. (1964). Circulatory response to submaximal and maximal exercise after thermal dehydration. *Journal of Applied Physiology,* **19**, 1125-1132.

Sargent, F. II, & Weinman, K.P. (1966). Eccrine sweat gland activity during the menstrual cycle. *Journal of Applied Physiology,* **21**, 1685-1687.

Sasaki, T. (1980). Effect of jet lag on sports performance. In L.E. Scheving & F. Halberg (Eds.), *Principles and application to shifts in schedules* (pp. 417-431). Rockville, MD: Sijthoff & Noordhof.

Savin, W.M., & Adams, W.C. (1979). Effects of ozone inhalation on work performance and $\dot{V}O_2$max. *Journal of Applied Physiology: Respiratory, Environmental, and Exercise Physiology,* **46**, 309-314.

Scholander, P.F., Hammel, H.T., Andersen, K.L., & Loyning, Y. (1958). Metabolic acclimation to cold in man. *Journal of Applied Physiology,* **12**, 1-8.

Scholander, P.F., Hammel, H.T., Hart, J.S., LeMessurier, D.H., & Steen, J. (1958). Cold adaptation in Australian aborigines. *Journal of Applied Physiology, 13*, 211-218.

Senay, L.C., Jr. (1979). Body fluids, exercise and hot climate. *Coach & Athlete, 51*(4), 18-19.

Sharkey, B.J. (1975). *Physiology and physical activity*. New York: Harper and Row.

Sheldahl, L.M., Buskirk, E.R., Loomis, J.L., Hodgson, J.L., & Mendez, J. (1982). Effects of exercise in cool water on body weight loss. *International Journal of Obesity, 6*, 29-42.

Sheppard, D., Saisho, A., Nadel, J.A., & Boushey, H.A. (1981). Exercise increases sulfur dioxide-induced bronchoconstriction in asthmatic subjects. *American Review of Respiratory Disease, 123*, 486-491.

Sheppard, D., Wong, W.S., Uehara, C.F., Nadel, J.A., & Boushey, H.A.. (1980). Lower threshold and greater bronchomotor responsiveness of asthmatic subjects to sulfur dioxide. *American Review of Respiratory Disease, 122*, 873-878.

Silverman, F., Folinsbee, L.J., Barnard, J., & Shephard, R.J. (1976). Pulmonary function changes in ozone—interaction of concentration and ventilation. *Journal of Applied Physiology, 41*, 859-864.

Skreslet, S., & Arefjord, F. (1968). Acclimatization to cold in man induced by frequent scuba diving in cold water. *Journal of Applied Physiology, 24*, 177-181.

Sloan, R.E.G., & Keatinge, W.R. (1975). Cooling rates of young people swimming in cold water. *Journal of Applied Physiology, 35*, 371-375.

Smith, R.M., & Hanna, J.M. (1975). Skinfolds and resting heat loss in cold air and water: Temperature equivalence. *Journal of Applied Physiology, 39*, 93-102.

Squires, R.W., & Buskirk, E.R. (1982). Aerobic capacity during acute exposure to simulated altitude, 914 to 2,286 meters. *Medicine and Science in Sports and Exercise, 14*, 36-40.

Standards Advisory Committee on Heat Stress. (1974, January 9). Recommended standard for work in hot environments. *Occupational Safety and Health Reporter*. Bureau of National Affairs, Inc.

Stiles, M.H. (1969). A first-hand report of the Mexico City Olympic Games. *Newsletter of the American College of Sports Medicine, 4*, 4-5.

Stromme, S., Andersen, K.L., & Elsner, R.W. (1963). Metabolic and thermal responses to muscular exertion in the cold. *Journal of Applied Physiology, 18*, 756-763.

Strydom, N.B., Wyndham, C.H., van Graan, C.H., Holdsworth, L.D., & Morrison, J.F. (1966). The influence of water restriction on the performance of men during a prolonged march. *South African Medical Journal, 40*, 539-544.

Vander, J.H., Sherman, J.H., & Luciano, D.S. (1975). *Human physiology: The mechanisms of body function* (2nd ed.). New York: McGraw-Hill.

Vanggaard, L. (1975). Physiological reactions to wet-cold. *Aviation, Space, and Environmental Medicine, 46*, 33-36.

Veicsteinas, A., Ferretti, G., & Rennie, D.W. (1982). Superficial shell insulation in resting and exercising men in cold water. *Journal of Applied Physiology: Respiratory, Environmental, and Exercise Physiology, 52*, 1557-1564.

Vogel, J.A., & Gleser, M.A. (1972). Effect of carbon monoxide on oxygen transport during exercise. *Journal of Applied Physiology, 32*, 234-239.

Vogel, J.A., Gleser, M.A., Wheeler, R.C., & Whitten, B.K. (1972). Carbon monoxide and physical work capacity. *Archives of Environmental Health, 24*, 198-203.

Vogel, J.A., & Hansen, J.E. (1967). Cardiovascular function during exercise at high altitude. In *The International Symposium on the Effects of Altitude on Physical Performance*. Chicago: The Athletic Institute.

Wagner, J.A., Horvath, S.M., Andrew, G.M., Cottle, W.H., & Bedi, J.F. (1978). Hypoxia, smoking history, and exercise. *Aviation, Space, and Environmental Medicine*, **49**, 785-791.

Wagner, J.A., Robinson, S., Tzankoff, S.P., & Marino, R.P. (1972). Heat tolerance and acclimatization to work in the heat in relation to age. *Journal of Applied Physiology*, **33**, 616-622.

Wayne, W.S., Wehrle, P.F., & Carroll, R.E. (1967). Oxidant air pollution and athletic performance. *Journal of the American Medical Association*, **199**, 901-904.

Weinman, K.P., Slabochova, Z., Bernauer, E.M., Morimoto, T., & Sargent, F. II. (1967). Reactions of men and women to repeated exposure to humid heat. *Journal of Applied Physiology*, **22**, 533-538.

Weiser, P.C., Morrill, C.G., Dickey, D.W., Kurt, T.L., & Cropp, G.J.A. (1978). Effects of low-level carbon monoxide exposure on the adaptation of healthy young men to aerobic work at an altitude of 1,610 meters. In L.J. Folinsbee, J.A. Wagner, J.F. Borgia, B.L. Drinkwater, J.A. Gliner & J.F. Bedi (Eds.), *Environmental stress: Individual human adaptations*. New York: Academic Press.

Wells, C.L. (1980). Physiological effects of a hot environment upon physical performance. In G.A. Stull (Ed.), *Encyclopedia of Physical Education, Fitness, and Sports: Training, Environment, Nutrition, and Fitness* (pp. 123-139). Salt Lake City: Brighton Publishing Co.

Wells, C.L. (1977). Sexual differences in heat stress response. *The Physician and Sportsmedicine*, **5**(9), 79-90.

Wells, C.L., & Horvath, S.M. (1973). Heat stress responses related to the menstrual cycle. *Journal of Applied Physiology*, **35**, 1-5.

Wells, C.L., & Horvath, S.M. (1974). Metabolic and thermoregulatory responses of women to exercise in two thermal environments. *Medicine and Science in Sports*, **6**, 8-13.

Wells, C.L., & Paolone, A.M. (1977). Metabolic responses to exercise in three thermal environments. *Aviation, Space, and Environmental Medicine*, **48**, 989-993.

West, J.B. (1982). Diffusion at high altitude. *Federation Proceedings*, **41**, 2128-2130.

Williams, M.H., Wesseldine, S., Somma, T., & Schuster, R. (1981). The effect of induced erythrocythemia upon 5-mile treadmill run time. *Medicine and Science in Sports and Exercise*, **13**, 169-175.

Wright, J.E., Vogel, J.A., Sampson, J.B., Knapik, J.J., Patton, J.F., & Daniels, W.L. (1983). Effects of travel across time zones (jet-lag) on exercise capacity and performance. *Aviation, Space, and Environmental Medicine*, **54**, 132-137.

Wyndham, C.H., Morrison, J.R., & Williams, C.G. (1965). Heat reactions of male and female Caucasians. *Journal of Applied Physiology*, **20**, 357-364.

Wyndham, C.H., Morrison, J.F., Williams, C.G., Bredell, G.A.G., Peter, J., Von Rahden, M.J.E., Holdsworth, L.D., Van Graan, C.H., Van Rensburg, A.J., & Munro, A. (1964). Physiological reactions to cold of Caucasian females. *Journal of Applied Physiology*, **19**, 877-880.

Wyndham, C.H., Plotkin, R., & Munro, A. (1964). Physiological reactions to cold of man in the Antarctic. *Journal of Applied Physiology*, **19**, 593-597.

Wyndham, C.H., & Strydom, N.B. (1969). The danger of an inadequate water intake during marathon running. *South African Medical Journal,* **43**, 893-896.

Young, A., Wright, J., Knapik, J., & Cymerman, A. (1980). Skeletal muscle strength during exposure to hypobaric hypoxia. *Medicine and Science in Sports and Exercise,* **12**, 330-335.

Young, A.J., Evans, W.J., Cymerman, A. Pandolf, K.B., Knapik, J.J., & Mahler, J.T. (1982). Sparing effect of chronic high-altitude exposure on muscle gycogen utilization. *Journal of Applied Physiology: Respiratory, Environmental, Exercise Physiology,* **52**, 857-862.

Index

A

Acclimatization 26, 37-40, 62-64, 81-82, 118, 120, 131
Acclimatization to heat 20, 23, 26, 37-40
Acute mountain sickness 83, 88, 118
Adaptation 1
ADH 18, 41, 50-51
Airway resistance 102-104, 107
Alcohol 64-65, 120
Aldosterone 18-19, 38, 40
Alkalosis 18
American Academy of Pediatrics 26
American College of Sports Medicine (ACSM) 31, 41
Antidiuretic hormone (ADH) 18-19, 50-51
Apocrine sweat glands 16
Artificial surfaces 40

B

Barometric pressure 70, 72, 77, 86
Basal metabolism 63
Black body 6
Blood flow 14-15, 22, 23-25, 32, 52, 56, 58, 64-65, 68, 74-75
Blood pressure 15-16, 18

Blood volume 17-18, 33, 81, 89
Body composition 20
Bronchoconstriction 102-104, 107

C

Carbon dioxide 9, 18, 23, 75-77, 81-83, 89
Carbon monoxide 94-97, 98-102, 105-107, 110-114
Cardiac output 15-16, 19, 24-26, 33, 40, 48-49, 66, 75, 77-78, 89, 99,
    105, 111
Cardiovascular 23-26, 31, 41
Cardiovascular fitness 23-25, 58, 66
Cerebral edema 84, 119
Chemoreceptors 72, 82, 89, 100
Children 25-27, 41, 84, 110
Chloride 17, 34
Circadian rhythms 4, 121-126
Clothing 6, 19-20, 27, 40, 44, 59-62, 119-120, 132
Cold 23
Conduction 5-7, 10, 15-16, 21, 25, 45, 54
Conductors 6-7
Conforming organisms 2-3
Convection 5, 7-8, 10, 15-16, 22, 23, 25, 44-45, 52, 54, 61
Core-shell concept 14-15
Core-skin temperature gradient 9
Core temperature 20
Countercurrent heat exchange 8, 23, 48, 64
Critical temperature 20

D

Dehydration 17-18, 26, 33-36, 76, 119-120, 131, 133
Diffusion capacity 79, 81, 85, 99, 106
Diphosphoglycerate (2, 3 DPG) 75, 81
Distance events 85-87
Diuresis 50-51
Diurnal 4
Dry bulb temperature 27, 31

E

Eccrine sweat 13
Ecology 2
Ecosystem 2
Effector mechanisms 4, 10, 14, 21, 27, 40
Electrolytes 8, 9, 18, 33-36, 38, 41
Endurance 23-24, 32, 41
Estrogen 25
Evaporation 5, 8-10, 16, 20-23, 44, 52
Exercise 15, 16, 22-24, 27, 33-35, 40
Exercise tolerance 23-24

F

Fasting 124
Fat 7
Fatigue 23, 38, 65-67, 77
Fatty acids 47, 53-54
Fever 4
Fluid balance 18
Fluid replacement 26-27, 32-35, 36-38 41, 76, 120, 132
Frostbite 49, 61-65, 85, 119

G

Gastric emptying 35
Globe temperature 6, 31
Glomerular filtration rate 18, 50
Glucose 34-36, 41
Guidelines 26-27, 31, 38-40

H

Heart rate 15-16, 18, 24-25, 36-39, 48-49, 52-54, 66, 75, 78, 80, 109,
    111, 121
Heat exchange 5, 10, 40

exhaustion 29, 31, 33, 118, 132-133
dissipation 13
injury 25, 27-31, 41
production 5, 20, 22
storage 5, 44, 46, 62
stress 13-14, 130
stroke 30-31, 131, 133
tolerance 9, 16, 23-25
Hemoconcentration 78
Hemoglobin 74-76, 81, 89-90, 99-102
Homeostasis 2, 14
Homeotherm 2, 20
Human thermostat 1, 3, 13
Humidity 8-9, 16, 21, 23, 26, 31, 44
Hydrocarbons 94
Hyperthermia 18, 30, 129, 131-135
Hypoglycemia 64-65, 132
Hypothalamus 3-4, 14, 16, 33, 35, 50, 133
Hypothermia 64-65, 85, 119, 129-135
Hypoxemia 81

I

Insulation 7, 20, 44-48, 52, 55-57, 59-62, 63, 65

J

Jet lag 121-126

K

Kidney 18

L

Lactic acid 23-24, 55, 66, 80, 105
Latent heat of vaporization 8

M

Maximum oxygen uptake 24, 57, 66, 77-79, 81, 85, 88-90, 105, 108-109, 111, 113, 120
Menstrual 4
Menstrual cycle 5, 25
Metabolic heat production 5, 20, 22, 44-46, 55, 57-58, 62-63, 65
Metabolism 5, 20, 22-23
Muscle 7, 22
Muscular endurance 67-68, 88, 123

N

Nitrogen dioxide 94-97, 103-104, 108, 110
Nonshivering thermogenesis 47, 63

O

Occupational Safety and Health Association (OSHA) 31, 41
Oxygen breathing 80, 84, 102
Oxygen dissociation curve 66, 72-76, 81, 100
Oxygen pressure (PO_2) 71, 77, 79-80, 89, 100
Oxygen uptake 5, 24, 44, 54, 66, 80, 85, 99, 105
Ozone 94-97, 99, 104-105, 108, 114

P

Particulates 94-97, 103, 107
Peroxyacetyl nitrate (PAN) 94, 105, 109-111
Perspiration 8
Plasma 15, 16-17, 33, 38
Plasma volume 18, 38, 51, 75, 81, 89
Poikilotherm 2
Polycythemia 81, 85
Polypropylene 9
Potassium 17, 34
Power events 66-67, 87-88

Pulmonary edema 84, 103, 119
Pyrogen 4

R

Radiant heat 17
Radiation 5-6, 10, 15-16, 21-23, 25, 40, 44
Regulating organisms 2, 3
Relative humidity 8-9, 16, 26, 31
Respiration 8, 18, 81-82
Respiratory alkalosis 77
Respiratory exchange ratio 53
Respiratory tract 8
Retinal hemorrhage 84

S

Set-point 4, 10
Sexual differences 24-25, 57-58, 64
Shivering 4-5, 22, 46-47, 50, 52, 54, 62-65, 133-134
Skin receptors 3-4
Skin temperature 16, 22, 23, 25, 50
Sleep 82-83, 123-124
Smog 95-98, 104, 109, 111
Sodium 17, 29, 33-34, 38
Solar radiation 21-22, 40, 71, 120, 130
Sprinting events 87
Strength 66-67, 88, 123
Stroke volume 16, 18-19, 24-25, 48-49, 52, 54, 66, 78, 81, 89, 99
Subcutaneous tissue 23
Sugar 35
Sulfur dioxide 94-99, 102-103, 107, 110
Sulfuric acid 94, 98, 103
Surface area/mass ratio 25-26, 50, 57
Sweating 8-10, 16-18, 20, 22-26, 33-34, 36-37, 44, 60, 119, 132-133
Sweat glands 16-18, 24, 26, 33
Syncope 18, 28, 31, 40, 132

T

Temperature, ambient 16, 20-21, 25-27, 44-45
   core 2-3, 5, 22-23, 36-39, 46, 48, 50-54, 56-58, 62, 64-65, 121-123

globe see Globe temperature
human 2
muscle 2, 55-56, 66-68
regulation 3
skin 16, 22-23, 25, 37-39, 44-46, 48-50, 52-55, 57-58, 61-64, 68
Testosterone 25
Thermal balance 5
 conductivity 6
 gradient 6, 15-16, 18, 22
 neutrality 20-21
Thermogenesis 46, 50, 52, 62
Thermoreceptors 3-4
Thermoregulation 3, 20, 49
Thirst 35-36
Total body water 17, 76, 133

U

Urine 15, 18, 50-51, 83

V

Vapor barrier 9-10
Vapor pressure 9, 22
Vasoconstriction 4, 14, 20, 47-48, 50-51, 58, 62
Vasodilatation 14-16, 20, 40, 48-49, 65
Vasodilation 4
Vasomotor 14
Ventilation 8, 18, 44, 78, 80-82, 89, 107-109
Venous return 16, 24, 51-52, 66, 81
Viscosity 7, 18, 67, 72, 75, 78, 81, 89

W

Water 9, 18, 31-36, 76, 130
Water immersion 45, 54-55, 60
Water replacement 18, 32-33, 34-35
Wet bulb 27, 31
Wet bulb globe temperature (WBGT) 31, 130, 134
Wind 8, 10, 44, 61-62, 64, 133
Wind chill index 8, 61, 65, 119
Women 24, 41

Z

Zeitgebers 121, 124-126
Zone of thermal neutrality 20-21